THE MASS

Prayer

THE MASS
As It Was, and Is and May Be

Mary Hester Valentine

THE THOMAS MORE PRESS
Chicago, Illinois

#24647623

ACKNOWLEDGMENTS

The author wishes to thank the *Catholic Herald* of Milwaukee for permission to quote from the column by Archbishop Weakland. And thanks also to *America* for permission to include citations from Walter M. Abbot's translation of the Documents of Vatican II.

ISBN 0-88347-265-1

CONTENTS

To the Mount Mary College Community
who gave me time, and
to Dan Herr and Joel Wells
who suggested I write this book

INTRODUCTION

WHILE the "Pastoral Constitution on the Church in the Modern World" *(Gaudium et Spes)* may well be the most all-embracing document of Vatican II, the "Constitution of the Sacred Liturgy," *(Sacrosanctum Concilium)* not only appears to have had the greatest impact on the individual Catholic, but has been the cause of the greatest controversy and disagreement. Twenty years after its proclamation, it is still a "sign of contradiction," not only among the laity, but within the ranks of the clergy, and even, at least one member of the hierarchy. Newspapers have covered every aspect of Archbishop Marcel Lefebvre's schismatic break with the Church, one of which was his insistence on the primacy of the Tridentine Mass, and its sacrificial emphasis.

In the United States Rev. George A. Stallings, now Bishop Stallings, has recently founded the *Imami* (faith in Swahili) Temple, which he claims will better meet the spiritual and cultural needs of Afro-Americans. In his first Mass, celebrated at Howard University Law School, the Sunday service, as reported by the New York *Times,* began with an entrance procession that included one participant wearing dreadlocks, and others who shook bells and rattles traditionally used in African ceremonies. The Mass itself included Catholic prayers and liturgy, along with words borrowed from African and Southern black revival traditions. Stallings preached, danced, and sang in the sanctuary at the front of the church, surrounded by aids, acolytes, and a gospel choir. The plywood altar was draped in the black, red and green colors used by organizations calling themselves Afro-American. At one point Stallings chanted, "We can't wait. How much longer does the Catholic Church need?"

While Cardinal James Hickey of Washington has condemned Stallings' new church, now that he has been consecrated Bishop there is little hope the ban will be lifted. However, the North American Bishops at their fall, 1989, meeting in Baltimore, did address themselves in a significant way to the liturgical needs of the Afro-American Catholics.

The Bishops of India have already made adaptations, approved by Rome, which are more in conformity with their culture, and there will doubtless be other changes in various non-Western churches. Thomas Smith, reflecting on a visit to Germany for the international meeting of Catholic journalists, noted that services in cathedrals in Cologne and Mainz, both of which were "awesome," still reflect the age in which the Cathedrals were built; the 7th to 10th centuries. The parish churches he found even more unusual, since it was obvious that post-Vatican II liturgical recommendations regarding statuary, vigil lights and communion rails were not being enforced by the German hierarchy, although the concelebrated Eucharistic liturgy for the World Congress of the Catholic Press had "two adorable girls," among the retinue of servers.

This diversity, even inconsistency, is familiar to American Catholics, and there are few weeks in which some less spectacular but equally strong reaction to liturgical change does not appear both in secular and diocesan papers. The problems seem to be more frequently voiced by traditionalists. Congregations are bitterly divided about a proposed removal of a marble communion rail; others are upset by the possibility of germs being spread through the Congregation's drinking from the same chalice, and others, including a correspondent who wrote dear Abby to say that he had been a devout Catholic from birth, but became a Protestant when the sign of peace, (shaking hands with the people around) was introduced into the liturgy of the Mass, since "hands are an incredible repository of germs."

This would all be petty, did it not involve the ignoring of what is central to the celebration of the Mass, concentrating instead on external rites, any one of which might be changed with no significant loss.

Humankind's historical records: —artifacts found

in archeological digs, cave drawings in Spain, France and Africa, the sacred maise of the Navajo, temple towers dating back to 3000 BC in southern Mesopotamia, religious figurines found in the Indus valley from about 2550 BC, and the more familiar Hellenistic records from 336 BC—all attest to the enduring need people have had over the ages to relate to a creator. Whatever the ritual, it was always a gathering of the community, be it the tribe or especially chosen members of the tribe who performed the function for the larger group. The Old Testament records not only the detailed regulations for the Hebrew sacrifice to Yahweh, but also the proscribed cults of the neighboring Caanite peoples. Danielou noted that only very lately archeological discoveries in Canaan have come to confirm not only the offering to the gods of bloody sacrifices, but also of bread and wine. He quotes M. Lods, who found evidence that the Caanites made libations. Many cups have been found that were used for the purpose. They also brought vegetable offerings, particularly loaves or cakes, which could, if need be, be replaced by baked rolls of earth, made in the same shape. Hundreds such have been found in the sanctuaries of Beisan.

The great high holy day of the Jews, the Passover, even today, is basically a memorial thanksgiving service to the God who freed their ancestors from slavery in Egypt.

THE MASS

And the Mass? It is the Catholic community's worship ceremony, a Eucharist, a thanksgiving performed for almost two millenia in response to Jesus, the God Man's final words at the Last Supper when he changed the Passover bread and wine into his flesh and blood, gave it to his disciples, ending the feast with the poignant request, "Do this in memory of me." Christ instituted the mystery of the Mass; it is not, therefore, something we can ignore at whim; it is the essential core of our religious life.

Romano Guardini, a decade or so before Vatican II, stressed the fact that the words the Lord used to establish the Mass are not, "Say this in memory of me, but *do* this in memory of me." Every one present is called to share in that happening. Up to a certain point we can understand the nature of the Mass by studying or reading books on the liturgy. But the act, the doing in Jesus' memory is ours only when we also *do*. It does not take much reflection for us to realize that we can do a thing, and still put very little of ourselves into it. We even have a saying which summarizes this type of indifference: His heart isn't in it.

True participation obviously requires an attentive mind, an involvement that, often, we do not bring to Mass. For too long, and for too many of us attendance has been the objective, the fulfillment of an obligation. It is no wonder that young people brought up in this passive atmosphere are rejecting it with the by now threadbare explanation, "It doesn't do anything for me."

There is a certain validity in this complaint, and the solutions are not simple, nor can they be detached from the milieu in which we live. Parents who insist on attendance with, "As long as you are a member of this family, living in this house, you will go to Mass with us," are not facing up to the real problem. Bernard Lee believes that at the heart of Christian faith there is a nonrational element that cannot be conceptualized or turned into discursive speech, though it can and must be communicated.

It is Guardini, again, who points out that there is a resistance in today's society to office and order, to authority and constitutionality. Only the directly spontaneous experience is considered truly valid. Teachers of writing struggle with this tendency in their students, the invoking of a "writer's block," to explain sheer inertia. Perhaps the advice the writing teacher gives, "Write without inspiration. The very act will prime the pump of creativity," can be applied to the more sacred action of participating in the celebration of Mass: worship-generated worship in its deepest sense.

There is an intuitive way of knowing, an affective way of thinking which offers a subjective-experiential means to knowledge. Implicit in its concern for process content and fundamentally nonverbal in its mode of expression, it is at home in the world of chaos, antistructure and ambiguity. While holistic and sensuous in style, it is best suited for supporting the imagination, mystery and discovery. It is the artificial separation of these two modes of consciousness, the depreciation of some of the signative, conceptual and analytical aspects of life, and the benign neglect of the symbolic, mythical, imaginative and emotive aspects of life which have contributed to our present religious disaffection in the Western Church, affirms Lee.

The belief, however, that the only religious act of value is that which arises involuntarily from within, is erroneous. Most of our life consists of actions of conscious effort, of service and activities for which we do not work up emotional response. Life consists only partly of spontaneous acts.

Liturgy does have the potential to become a powerful means of raising our religious consciousness, but as Father John F. Egan has pointed out, if it is seen solely as that, we shall once again have distorted, if not destroyed it. We need to become aware that we are gathered as members of Christ's body, offering worship in and through him, and drawing our common life of grace from our union with him, a fostering of a profound consciousness of our dependence on one another in Christ.

The Council Fathers of Vatican II were acutely aware of the need to revitalize the Mass for the people of God. It was this concern that brought about the document on the liturgy with its openness to changes in the dead accretions and liturgical trivia which had developed over the centuries. And, oddly enough, it is the changes aimed at meeting modern needs which have been the divisive facets, both of those who would seal the past in the present, and for those who are restless with what they consider the slow pace of change.

This book will attempt to reveal where the Church is at this historical moment, and by studying its past, discover how it has arrived here. It will, I hope, point out that change in unessentials has been the one consistent pattern for the celebration of Mass from the early Apostolic age to the present. The insights the Church has developed over the centuries concerning the real presence of the Eucharistic Christ have also been extended to the people who are the real presence of Christ, as St. Paul learned on the way to Damascus when he heard the divine voice say, "I am Jesus whom you are persecuting."

A study of current teaching and doctrine will be an introduction to contemporary thinking and debate, with the potential for further changes the latter provides. Christ gave no detailed instructions on how the Mass was to be celebrated, a fact which has allowed the liturgy to be affected by the historical and cultural situation in which the specific congregations lived, their size and varied needs. But the essential remains untouched, and we must enter into it.

In a book this brief it is, of course, not possible to cover all the historical and cultural conditions which were the background for the varying emphases over the centuries. I will not take a devotional approach to the topic; the matter under consideration will be, for the most part, historical and I hope, objective. But if reading it does not provide the material out of which the individual believer is strengthened in his faith, and encouraged to bring to his participation at Mass the vital attitude needed to transform a collection of individuals into a congregation intent on worship and union with God, it has failed in its primary objective. For as Monica Hellwig insists, "The Eucharist is the center of all we do and are and hope as Christians."

TRADITION AND HISTORY

HAVE you ever wondered when the Apostles first did what Jesus had requested in memory of him, that is, when they gathered for the first time for a meal at which they said the sacred words which enabled the divine action to take place, and the bread become his body and the wine his blood? Not too many years ago a common First Communion certificate pictured St. John giving Our Lady Communion, a picture totally without historical justification, but certainly representing a possibility. We simply do not know when the first Mass was celebrated or by whom, after Christ's last appearance to his disciples following his resurrection.

We do know that the number of believers in Jesus as God exploded almost immediately, for Peter's preaching on Pentecost resulted in the conversion of 5,000, a number which may simply represent a crowd, but even if not statistically accurate, does indicate a phenomenal growth in the number of those for whom Jesus became the Way, the Truth, and the Life. *Acts* tell us that the Apostles, like their Master, continued to fulfill the Law, continued to go to the Temple to pray and to offer Sacrifice. SS. Peter and John cured the lame man at the Beautiful Gate on their way to pray in the temple (*Acts* 3:1-10) and St. Paul testified that he prayed in the synagogues in Damascus. (*Acts* 8:9)

The earliest believers clearly continued to see themselves as devout Jews, and continued to worship in the temple and to practice the Jewish ceremonials at prayer. But their belief in Jesus as God, and the experience they had of oneness in his Spirit led them to develop their own forms of common prayer. They began to gather in the homes of more prominent members of the community who were believers. (*Acts* 2:46; 5:42; 12:12) In fact, it was not until the 8th century that Christianity and Judaism were completely distinct.

Josef A. Jungmann, S.J., whose history of the Mass is a recognized scholarly study, insists that any history of the celebration of the Eucharist must begin with the Institution itself, two accounts of which exist: that of St. Paul (I *Cor.* 11: 20-26) and the reports in the synoptics (*Luke* 22:19 ff.; *Mark* 14:22-24, and *Matt.* 26:26 ff). Basil Pennington points out that we cannot know exactly what words our Lord used when he presented the bread-flesh and the cup of wine-blood to the twelve, since St. Paul has one formula and the three Synoptic Gospels each offer their own, and the formula that has come to be enshrined in the Roman Canon differs from all these scriptural texts. As a result, he notes that today we realize that the "mystery of faith" lies essentially in a sacramental and effective memorial rather than in a formula.

John Egan agrees, but adds that Christ was not only carrying out the Old Testament worship, and giving reality to what was there in figure, but in his own sacrifice he was taking up all together, and as it were, giving a new reality to all the sacrifices men had offered in all religions at all times. All the efforts ever made to worship God and enter into communion with him, which had never been fully able to achieve their end, were thus completed and perfected in Christ's sacrifice.

Obviously, the Eucharist of the Last Supper was surrounded by the rituals attached to the Passover meal. Raymond Brown, commenting on this, notes that the Jewish Christians could accept the Eucharist as a memorial, but might have some difficulty with John's eucharistic theology. According to Brown, the Synoptic and Pauline passages about the Last Supper associate the Eucharistic words of Jesus with the commemoration of his death. ". . . in memory of me." You proclaim the death of the Lord until he comes. Jewish Christians could understand a meal that recalls or makes present again the salvific action of the past, since the Passover meal itself was a recollection of the deliverance from Egypt. But as Father Brown observes, St. John interprets the Eucharist as the food and drink that gives eternal life, launching Christianity on the road to a distinctive sacramental theology, whereby visible elements are signs communicating divine realities.

It is in Chapter VI of John's Gospel that we find Jesus' own first reference to the gift he will give of himself at the Last Supper. "The bread that I shall give is my flesh for the life of the world," (John VI:51) echoed in Luke's report of the Last Supper (Luke XXII:19).

It is clear that in the early years after Christ's ascension the disciples became a little group distinct from, and yet still adhering to their Mosaic heritage. As Frederick Cwiekowski points out, evidence for the development of an independent community is quite thin, and the case for the beginnings of the community meals within which the Eucharist would develop is even thinner. To add to the problem, there is no clear agreement among critical scholars on the evaluation of such evidence as we do have. Dunn believes that in those earliest months and years there was no clear distinction in the minds of the believers between the fellowship meals and those in which they specifically recalled the words of the Last Supper. He suggests, furthermore, that at the very beginning the Lord's Supper may have been an annual celebration, a type of Christian Passover.

The question whether the Last Supper was a Passover meal or not is still not settled. If the Last Sup-

THE MASS

per was not a Passover meal, then its interpretation as such, even within the New Testament itself is, according to Osborne, already theologizing. It is clear, however, that the Eucharist was situated within a meal complex, and a Jewish meal rather than a Graeco-Roman one. At a Jewish meal the host figure was the main male figure of the, perhaps, wider Jewish family. This point alone raises the question of who might have presided at the early Eucharists. It is historically not at all clear today that in that earliest of Christian periods only an ordained person presided at the Eucharist. That ordination was required cannot be ascertained by the historical material in the New Testament. The issue of ministry in the New Testament is extremely complex, and the precise tasks of the presbyter are unclear and cannot be measured by the tasks of the priest today, as Osborne points out.

If we return to Paul's account which, according to most scholars is the oldest, since it appears to have been written around the year 54, it is interesting to note that the author was not present at the Last Supper. He was handing down information which was already a tradition, and may be traced to the Christian community of Antioch where Paul lived and preached about the year 44 (*Acts* 11:26).

His account was written to clarify for the Church of Corinth the meaning of what the rite of the Eucharist does. His account follows that of St. Luke, and seems to reflect most accurately the course of festive meals among the Jews. First the wine is made ready, and each of those present drinks in turn, as is done today at the Seder. This rite is accompanied by a prayer.

There are only a few scattered clues as to how the apostles actually fulfilled the mandate the Lord gave at the Last Supper, how they integrated the Institution of the Eucharist into the life of the early Church. Jungmann points out that we simply do not know how they decided in what framework and setting the memorial should be celebrated, on what occasions, and with what group of participants. The New Testament gives only incomplete answers, but one thing is very clear: the infant Church was conducting the celebration right from the beginning with surprising sureness, uniformity of rubrics and with the same literal, realistic interpretation.

The *Acts* bear witness to the breaking of bread in the first Christian community. "The bread we break" (*Cor.* 1:10-16) is obviously the Eucharist. So, too, nothing but the Eucharist could have been meant when the community of Troas "on the first day of the week . . . met for the breaking of bread." (*Acts* 20:7) We can only estimate the frequency of these early community gatherings. Based on the thought that these Christian groups followed the example of Jewish sabbath observance the best guess is that they were weekly, a presumption strengthened by Paul's directive to the Corinthians regarding the collection for the Jerusalem church (I Cor. 16:2).

The faithful of the young Church must have come together in little groups for a common evening meal in houses where there was a room suitable for it. Visitors to the Holy Land are shown archaeological evidence of these early church houses, the one in Nazareth probably being the most famous. Paul's letters tell us something of these assemblies (I Cor. 16:2). The faithful knew that at their gatherings, and especially when they celebrated the Eucharist, it was the Lord who was there in their midst as he himself had promised (*Matt.* 18:20).

Cwiekowski, discussing the beginnings of the Church calls attention to the fact that gathering for festive meals was a common feature of the life of the clubs, guilds and other voluntary associations that were a part of social life in the early Roman Empire. In Jewish culture, sharing a meal implied a bond of unity, a sharing of one's life. Table fellowship in Judaism then as now, implied fellowship before God. Those who shared the food shared in the blessing which the head of the household pronounced. All of this seems almost unnecessary to state, since eating together is an universal human practice. Today celebrations and gatherings traditionally include a meal. Believer and unbeliever share Rotarian dinners, fund-raising banquets, family anniversaries and Thanksgiving feasts.

The Eucharist is mentioned only in passing in the letter of Pope St. Clement to the community of Corinth, written at the end of the first century, A.D. Pliny, the Younger, reporting to the Emperor Trajan in 112, asked what his attitude was to be toward Christians who, he says, "habitually assemble on a set day, before sunrise and sing a hymn to Christ as to a god. . . . They go their ways and assemble again later on for their meal, which, whatever may be said of it, is ordinary and harmless."

The *Didache*, which goes back to about the same time, is the first Christian document dealing with the celebration of the Eucharist. In chapter 14 it says, "On the dominical day of the Lord, come together to break bread and give thanks, after having, in addition, confessed your sins so that your sacrifice may be pure. But let any one who is at odds with his fellow not join with you until he has first been reconciled, lest your sacrifice be profaned." This is an echo, certainly, of Christ's warning that we leave our gift at the altar if we remember a need for reconciliation, and only after that return to make the offering. In the *Didache* it is clearly a reference to the Eucharist.

Jungmann points out that by the second century the Eucharistic gathering became independent of the meal, a development which brought about a significant architectural decision: all the tables disappeared except the one on which the bread and wine were kept, and the dining hall became a place of religious assembly. Communities sufficiently well off acquired an ordinary house and adapted it to their needs. Later, in Rome, Christians contracted with an innkeeper to buy a house that was in the public domain, and Emperor Alexander Severus (222-65) gave them preference on the grounds that a place of worship was preferable to a bar!

In 304 when some of the faithful were being questioned before the imperial tribunal at Carthage, the proconsul asked one of them, "Was it in your house that the gathering was held?" and was answered, "Yes, it was in my house that we celebrated the *Dominicum*," a term that undoubtedly signifies the Eucharist.

All of these records show the importance and meaning of the Eucharistic assembly, but they hardly give any idea of how the actual celebration proceeded. We are, therefore, fortunate to have a little treatise known as the first *Apology*, which St. Justin addressed to Emperor Antoninus Pius (131-61). Chapter 67 provides a description of the Sunday assembly, while chapter 65 described the Eucharistic liturgy proper. Father John J. Egan finds it noteworthy that "when the prayers and Eucharist are finished the people present give their assent with an Amen," which in Hebrew means, "So be it."

St. Justin goes on to say that "Next, the gifts which have been eucharistified are distributed, and every one shares in them, while they are also sent via the deacons to the absent brethren." The Mass then continues with a fundamental structure which has lasted to our own day: the Liturgy of the Word, the readings, homily, and the consecration and communion. It is interesting to note that Justin refers to the mingling of water with the wine, a practice customary in the Palestine of Jesus' day.

After St. Justin, references to the Eucharist become more frequent. St. Irenaeus, reflecting on the essence of the Eucharist, points out that far from contradicting the Old Covenant this was its fulfillment. Clement and Origen of Alexandria are interested primarily in an allegorical interpretation of Church tradition, while St. Chrysostom will later speak of the manner in which the sacrifice comes about in the Eucharist: "It is not man that causes the offerings to become the body and blood of Christ, but Christ himself, acting through the priest.

Contrary to Dunn's belief that the celebration took place only annually at Passover, St. Cyprian seems to indicate that the Mass was celebrated daily in order that the faithful might "face the coming persecution, one must drink the chalice daily, and so be ready to shed one's own blood for Christ."

THE MASS

It is important today to recall that the Mass has been supremely important in the lives of our predecessors, since we are the sum of all our ancestors.

By the third century the ritual had begun to be formalized. The earliest dated Eucharistic prayer that resembles ours, according to Robert Cabie, goes back to about the year 215 and occurs in a document that scholars have identified with the Apostolic tradition of Hippolytus. The overall structure is familiar, and Cabie notes that the Bible was the only liturgical book. It became a binding custom throughout the Church that the final and climactic reading should be from the gospel, which sheds its light on the other readings which preceded it —a formula still followed today.

It is Cabie, too, who notes that the bishop was ordered to take great pains with the Sunday Eucharist, since it was a sign of the Church. "A special welcome is to be given to the poor, even if the bishop has to surrender his own chair and sit on the floor," a clear challenge to the divisions that run through human society, and did then as now.

Tertullian in the third century makes explicit mention of the Eucharistic celebration on the station days, Wednesday and Friday, and at the annual remembrance of the dead. Raymond Brown, further notes that "All those present receive Communion as a matter of course; so much so that if one does not intend to communicate, one must stay away from the celebration itself. Communion is distributed under both species; in fact, one may even take the Lord's body home, and eat it before all other food." At this period, part of the sacred bread was kept back after every Mass. A custom arose of receiving a piece of the sacred bread from a previous Mass to drop into the chalice at the next one, to signify that though time separated them, the Masses were one act of worship.

George Every does not believe that the problem of celebrating the Eucharist in time of persecution was made easier by the practice of communion at home. He refers to a practice which came under criticism, and was abolished entirely in the 4th century: that is, the pouring of wine over the bread, which was then considered consecrated by contact. Towards the end of the 4th century there were still Christians in Rome, who made their communion daily in their own bedroom, as soon as they got up in the morning. St. Jerome in his letter to Pammachius neither condemned nor approved the practice. But Tertullian warned his wife that if she married again after his martyrdom (he died in bed!) her pagan husband would want to know "what you taste secretly before all other food." But the principle of consecration by contact was not denied, although in the scholastic period later, it became a point of contention in the schools of Paris and elsewhere.

THE MASS

Many Catholics even today are convinced that in time of persecution the faithful used to gather in the catacombs to celebrate secretly. But contemporary scholars doubt that this was the usual thing, since catacombs were ill-suited for such a purpose. They were known to every one, and in most of them Christians were interred side by side with pagans, and the celebration of Mass might well be interrupted by a pagan funeral.

For those reluctant to give up the romantic picture of dark, damp catacombs, with flickering lanterns held by worshiping Christians, a picture most remember from early reading of *Fabiola*, there is some small scholarly justification for adhering to that heroic image. Richard Woods, O.P., states that under Roman law all cemeteries were sacrosanct. "Even those of the outlaw Christians were seldom violated by the police," he claims, and "as a fortunate consequence, not only did many liturgical rites develop in the catacombs, but the earliest examples of Christian art are found in their frescoes." They continued to be used, according to Woods, until the fifth century, when they were abandoned because of increasing barbarian attacks near the City.

Tertullian testified that the ritual was not to be performed outwardly only, but it should also be performed interiorly with a purifying confession at the beginning. The greeting, "The Lord be with you," or "Peace be with you," are both Hebraic forms of greeting used in the early community, and continued in today's liturgy, as is the traditional answer, "And with your spirit."

The invitation to prayer, "Let us pray," also has a parallel in Judaic prayer, as does the ratifying *Amen*. *Alleluia* and *Hosanna* are both Judaic, and the concluding doxology to formal prayer originated in the Synagogue.

In the early Church, following St. Paul's the redemptive suffering of Jesus as a sacrifice, (I Cor. 5:7) is reinforced by St. Peter's assertion that our ransom was not paid in silver or gold but in the blood of the spotless, unblemished Lamb (I Peter, 1:18-19).

It was the custom for the faithful to contribute bread and wine for the celebration. Eustachius of Constantinople preserves a fragment of St. Athanasius' sermon decribing this gift-giving. "You shall see the levites bring loaves and chalice of wine, and place them on the table. As long as the invocation and prayers have not begun there is only bread and wine. But after the great and wonderful prayers have been pronounced, then the bread becomes the body of our Lord, Jesus Christ, and the wine becomes his blood."

By this time, the third century, the Eucharist was no longer joined to a meal, and the celebration was shifted to a time outside working hours, for among

THE MASS

early Christians Sunday was officially as much a working day as any other. The most frequent choice was an early morning hour.

By that time, too, the liturgy of the Mass was adapted to a far larger building in which it was being celebrated, since the end of persecution made larger assemblies possible. As a result, two traditions developed: the Gregorian Sacramentary for functions at which the Pope presided, and the Gelasian for use in churches in which the celebrant was a priest. It was at this time, too, that with promotion of Bishops to official rank in the Roman empire, the liturgy took on forms of courtly ceremonial with lights, incense, and genuflections.

Popular participation, too, sometimes took on exuberant forms, so much so, that in their homilies, the Fathers, especially St. John Chrysostom, had to recall their congregations to order in the course of the celebration.

The 4th and 5th centuries were a period of intense creativity in the area of Eucharistic prayers. The Entrance hymn, for example, assumed a specific function as a kind of overture, to give the pitch and suggest the mood and tone of the celebration. The presider proposed intentions with specific objects, and the faithful responded with *Amen*—similar to the bidding prayers of today's Mass. The formulation of intentions was not fixed, although the form, like today's, followed a certain pattern.

Mary Hester Valentine

The formula, "Let us give thanks to the Lord," and the response, "It is right and just," originated in this period. Various churches created their respective traditions, some of which were later codified. At the end of the 7th century, for example, the *Agnus Dei* was introduced by the Syrian Pope, Sergius I. The sacramental meal, following the pattern of the Last Supper, was bread and wine. Bread has always been wheaten bread, since that was prescribed for the paschal meal. Almost universally, since the Passover was associated with the Feast of the Unleavened Bread, unleavened bread has been used in Mass in the Latin rite. But Jungmann points out that the Church has actually placed no great importance on the distinction between leavened and unleavened bread in the Eucharist, and over the centuries both have been used. There are studies currently being conducted about the possibility of other grains being used in countries where wheat is rare and the price prohibitive. I will discuss the possibility of this change later.

Wine was to be obtained from grapes, but until Trent no detailed regulations regarding quality or color had been laid down. In some churches in the early centuries, there was a tendency to use water instead of wine, but St. Cyprian put this down with a strong, disapproving voice. Clearly the real presence of Jesus in the Eucharist is a constant, not only in the New Testament, but also in the history of the

Church. There were no Eucharistic heresies of any note until the 9th century. This alone indicates a widespread unity on the issue of the real presence.

The attitude of the communicant is carefully described in the Jerusalem *Catecheses:* "When you approach do not extend your hands with palms upward and fingers apart, but make your left hand a throne for your right hand, since the latter is to receive the King; then, while answering *Amen,* receive the body of Christ in the hollow of your hand." These directives sound very contemporary as does St. Ambrose's, "Not without reason do you say *Amen,* for you acknowledge in your heart that you are receiving the body of Christ. Let the heart persevere in what the tongue confesses."

The custom of receiving Communion on the tongue was introduced about the time the use of unleavened bread became general in the West (11th century), a custom which probably led to the practice of kneeling to receive Communion, since this made it easier for the priest to put the host in the mouth. But by the 13th century, unfortunately, for reasons too complicated to describe briefly, the faithful rarely received Communion, and the elevation of the host after the consecration was introduced to allow them to see the Body of Christ.

Singing during the celebration is referred to by St. Paul, and from that earliest period has remained a part of the Eucharistic celebration. The *Kyrie,*

Mary Hester Valentine

Gloria, Sanctus, and *Agnus Dei,* which were introduced at different times, were always choral hymns, meant to be sung by the entire congregation, and only when this was not feasible, by a choir. Originally the *schola* consisted of the clergy assisting at the Mass, but over the centuries performance became more musically sophisticated.

The early plain chant, commonly called Gregorian in honor of Gregory the Great, to whom tradition ascribes its final arrangement, was composed before the year 600, according to modern authorities, including Benedictine musicologists. Most of the manuscripts still in existence are from the 13th to the 16th centuries, although there is an incomplete manuscript from the 12th century in the British museum. While it did not remain the only music sung during the Mass, it remained standard even into the 20th century. Most Catholics old enough to remember Mass before Vatican II also remember Gregorian chant, chiefly from the Requiem Masses, which in all too many cases were the parish Mass, requested as memorial for a loved one. For those interested in ancient ecclesiastical music the Antiphony of Bangor may be a fascinating study. It appears to have been compiled in that monastery between 680-691, and was taken from Ireland to Bobbio. It is now in Milan in the Ambrosiana Library, where it was removed in 1609 by Frederigo Borromeo. The hymn may well be much earlier than the date of the Antiphonary, although the legend which associates it with St. Patrick is untenable.

By the end of the Middle Ages polyphony was introduced, music which imposed greater demands on the singers' talents and training, so that qualified lay persons had to be engaged. Professional choirs became the norm for solemn occasions. When women were admitted into the choir, architectual changes in the churches were introduced. Since women were not permitted into the sanctuary, choir lofts were erected.

There was some objection to the entertainment quality being added to the Mass. St. Bernard of Clairvaux warned against the danger of increasing secularization inherent in the development, and even earlier, St. Gregory the Great in the Roman Synod of 505 abolished the practice of choosing deacons solely for their fine voices.

Palestrina in the 16th century inaugurated a polyphony, for which, besides the organ, the whole range of orchestral instruments was increasingly pressed into service. Jungmann notes that if this music had served to adorn only an occasional feast-day Mass in the cathedral, the increased solemnity might have been well worth it. The regrettable thing was that now elegant musical service was attempted Sunday after Sunday in both city and country parishes, and the Mass lost its primary purpose of communal sharing of the Lord's supper. By the 15th century, according to Every, music excited more desire than devotion. Battle and hunting songs were sung. Traces of this entertainment appeal persisted into the 20th century, and I can recall being advised to attend a certain church in Germany, because their Sunday Mass had such a beautiful choir with orchestral accompaniment, and the week I was to be in town a famous soprano was scheduled to sing some of the solo parts. This never had universal appeal, and there were always critics in every century who continued to preach the core of the Mass.

As liturgy developed, a parallel shift became apparent in the theology of the Eucharist. Early debate, arguments, heresies, had for the most part, dealt with the person of Christ: his divinity and humanity with various interpretations. Rarely was the Eucharist the subject of much heated debate, although some controversy, even before the Reformation revolved around the question as to whether the bread and wine became the body and blood of Christ, or merely symbolized it, or the recurring debate as to whether Christ was present to the communicant only at the moment of reception, or whether he remained also in the consecrated host in the tabernacle.

In the Eastern liturgies the concept of sacrifice not only received special emphasis, but was characterized by a distinctive approach as well. The Christian sacrifice is a mystery, a mystical event. The act of dismissing those not permitted to participate (specifically the catechumens) was accepted as a matter of course as early as Tertullian. In the Byzantine liturgy the dismissal of catechumens is retained as a ritual even to this day. But then, to this rite another element of secrecy had been introduced into the celebration: the sacred parts of the Mass were not to be performed in the presence of even the faithful permitted to gather there.

Theologians during the Middle Ages seemed content to reflect on what had been inherited from the teaching of the Church Fathers. For St. Augustine the special power of the Eucharist consists in this: our union with the sacrifice that Christ has offered and still offers. As Jungmann notes, Augustine's special achievement is that, beyond mere ritualism, he stressed strongly the symbolic meaning underlying the Eucharist.

When Latin ceased to be a living language, about the 9th century, the liturgy became essentially a monopoly of the clergy. It was then especially that the controversy over Consecration arose: whether the actual, historical body of Christ was present in the Eucharist, or whether the bread and wine were only its symbol, with which some power of God was associated.

About the year 1200 the ideas clarified began to

be expressed in the ritual of the Mass, and it became the custom to raise the host for veneration of the faithful after the Consecration. St. Thomas Aquinas focused on the question of the nature of the sacrament and the Real Presence, noting that Mass is "both offered as a sacrifice and consecrated and received as a sacrament." According to him, the priest consecrates "in the name and through the power of Christ, so that Christ is in a special manner also the celebrant." Thomas Aquinas was the first to state that the separate consecration of the two species represented the separation of Christ's body and blood in his Passion, although this is implied in Matthew's version of the Institution at the Last Supper. (Matt. 26:26-28). It was at this time that the term, based on Aristotelian philosophy, began to appear in discussion of the Mass: transubstantiation. It has remained a stumbling block until very recently for any ecumenical dialogue to be fruitful, since the Reformers objected to the word. Contemporary Roman Catholic theologians have also, for the most part, ceased to use it, substituting other terms which to the layman are not particularly significant.

In the mid-13th century the feast of Corpus Christi was introduced, bringing with it the procession of the Blessed Sacrament, exposition, and the Benediction Service. There was a concentration of the cult of the Eucharist within and outside the Mass, rather than on the celebration of the Eucharist and the people's participation in it.

As a result, devotion to the Mass often took a distorted form. From participation in the Mass, or even from a glimpse of the elevated host, people hoped both for spiritual graces and earthly advantages: on that day one would not die a sudden death, or would not become blind, deaf or dumb. There was also a popular superstition that through every Mass one soul would be freed from purgatory. It is important to note that the official theology of the time did not advocate or defend these beliefs. In fact, Cabie emphasizes that the Church had to react against these popular customs which, when not infected with superstition, focused on superficial, secondary aspects of the Mass.

By the beginning of the 16th century many pastors felt that a renewal of the Eucharist was an urgent necessity for the faithful. The multiplication of Masses for special intentions became extreme, with almost no thought of a celebrating community. Of course, there were always some who protested against excessive multiplication of Masses; Francis of Assisi urged his brothers to celebrate Mass only once a day.

Another abuse, dangerously close to simony, arose from the practice of offering the priest a stipend for a memorial Mass to be said for the donor's intention. The Church for many centuries had been careful to lay down detailed regulations governing these offerings, but the abuses to which the practice lent itself were not unknown, even recently. Since all grace is by nature a free gift of God, the stipend does not entitle the giver to the fruits of the Mass, but simply binds the priest to pray for him during the sacrifice.

Erasmus, in his *De Sarcienda Ecclegiae Concordia* fumes against these abuses. "There is the Mass of the crown of thorns, of the three nails. Masses for those who travel by land and sea, for barren women, for persons sick of quartan and tertian fevers." And later he reproves the insolence of those who walk about the church when Mass is being celebrated, talking of their own private affairs, and when it is finished, go and find a priest of their own to say a special Mass for them.

George Every reports that people often brought hawks, falcons, and dogs to church, and priests chatted in vestments, leaving their birettas and gloves on the altar. Mass was sometimes celebrated at the corners of streets, after midnight feasts, especially after weddings, in the bridal chamber. It is no wonder, then, that details concerning the celebration of the Mass were a central concern of the Council of Trent in 1514. The decisions made were to have long-lasting effects, not all of which were what the Council Fathers had in mind. Appeals for the use of the vernacular in the Mass, so that the faithful might once again be active participants were rejected. The Fathers did not think it should be celebrated in the vernacular "indiscriminately." The use of the adverb here is significant, since it obviously indicates, what even scholars writing on the strictures of the Council, frequently ignore: the vernacular was not ruled out absolutely, although in matter of fact, its use was limited almost exclusively to Uniate churches. The Council was seriously concerned about instruction of the faithful, and pastors were ordered to explain the readings during the Mass, and the mystery of the holy sacrifice itself.

The Roman Missal, revised by the Council of Trent, was promulgated in a Bull of July 14, 1570. Valuable changes had been made; many feasts of the saints were dropped from the liturgical cycle so that the Church year could concentrate on the major feasts of Christ's life. The elaborate music, some of which was sung even during the Canon, was limited, and music was restricted to the ancient liturgical *Kyrie, Gloria,* Creed, *Sanctus* and *Agnus Dei,* and the priest's call to praise.

It was a noble effort, and a too simple criticism of the Roman Missal of Pius V disregards the exaggerations and popular superstitions with which the Council of Trent had to deal. Unfortunately for succeeding centuries, however, some unintentional results grew out of the new ritual.

One of the urgent problems facing the Council Fathers was to control the celebration of Mass by priests of little education, whose conduct frequently gave rise to concern. George Every points out that the desire to provide them with meticulous regulations for every detail of their behavior in church resulted in a rigidity which would increase as printed Missals prescribed not only every prayer but every gesture, and in some, for instance the *Ordo Missae* of John Burchard, there was an attempt to regulate the behavior of those who attended Mass, indicating when they should stand or kneel.

The use of Latin, which by the 16th century had become a dead language except for the literate few, prevented the ordinary layman from an intelligent participation in the responses and prayers. Informed participation in the Mass declined, and the belief slowly slid into the common consciousness, including the 20th century, that what was required of the faithful was only that they be present and "hear" the Mass. It would be wrong to say that because of this the majority of those fulfilling their Sunday Mass obligation were not worshiping God.

THE MASS

The devotion of the faithful, however, was directed more often toward the veneration of the Sacrament than toward the co-offering of the Mass. Mass had ceased to be a sacred communal meal; in fact until Vatican II, Communion was administered before Mass in many parishes, so that those who could not stay for the Mass could receive Christ, a devotional practice which completely separated Communion from its part in the Eucharistic meal, a meal which sanctifies man. There was obviously, a development here of the erroneous idea that the Mass is primarily a way of consecrating the host for adoration and communion.

This Communion-centered spirituality encouraged private thanksgiving as a kind of substitute for the brevity of the postcommunion ceremony of the Mass. St. Alphonsus Liguori prescribed at least a half hour of thanksgiving after Communion. I recall a biologically-minded priest telling first-communicants that since it took about fifteen minutes for the host to be absorbed into their blood-stream (I don't know his scientific source) they should talk to Jesus in their hearts for a quarter of an hour. What he forgot to tell them was that Jesus is within us at all times, as he himself has assured us.

At any rate, the Tridentine Missal of Pius V gave the Order of the Mass a new form that would put its stamp on the Roman rite for centuries to come, a

45

complication for those concerned liturgists who saw that the emphasis on rubrics was separating the faithful from the Eucharistic meal. Much needed changes were rejected on the basis that the Bull of 1570 expressly stipulated that nothing should be changed.

This was obviously a misreading of the document. There was never any intention of making the Missal of Pius V the sole legitimate liturgical expression for all ages to come. Every Council realizes that its decisions not dealing directly with dogma can be changed, and have been many times over the centuries, to correspond to changing circumstances and needs. Cabie points out that two new editions of the Tridentine book appeared in the 17th century, in 1604 under Clement VII and in 1634 under Urban VIII, and both introduced changes.

In fact, Pierre Loret notes that historians have always wondered whether Pius V himself ever used his own missal. Being a Dominican as well as Pope, it is possible he continued to celebrate Mass according to the Dominican liturgy, a rite fulfilling the requirement of being an approved liturgy at least 200 years old at the time of the Council of Trent.

In the meantime, the Congregation of Rites appointed by Pope Sixtus V to watch over the liturgy, refined fine points to a degree approaching ecclesiastical trivia. For example, books were written detailing the shape of the tabernacle or the length of the altar cloth, directing the deacon when he presented the paten or the chalice to the celebrant to first kiss the object, then the hand of the celebrant, or at the offertory blessing to receive the incense boat with his right hand, then transfer it to his left, to present the celebrant the spoon for the incense with his right hand, kissing the end the celebrant will take, and then kissing the celebrant's hand. As Loret wryly comments, "Any one who has done this knows how fast he has to move," and ends with, "they did not leave out a thing." Obviously rubrics had descended to the ludicrous and liturgical reform was inevitable.

In our own century, even before Vatican II, St. Pius X revised the Roman Missal in 1914, after having promulgated a new edition of the *Graduale Romanum* in 1907. In 1909 he published the well-known decree on frequent and even daily communion. He might have introduced more radical changes had he lived longer, an amusing possibility, since he is best remembered by American catholics as the Pope who fought Modernism in the Church.

Liturgists have always held, as John Meagher has indicated, that in reforming established practices it is better to stay within the tradition where possible. But sometimes interpretations must be newly constructed where the tradition is insufficient, "as in the modern proposals to reinterpret Catholic understanding of Eucharistic consecration as transignification . . . to make up for what transubstantiation lost its capacity to accomplish, once the Scholastic-philosophical-theological framework could no longer be assumed."

LITURGY AND VATICAN II

IT IS an interesting commentary on the average Catholic's uncritical observance of the Mass as he knew it, that the changes in the 20th century, both before Vatican II and that body's *Constitution on the Sacred Liturgy* caught him almost completely by surprise. Actually, liturgists had been studying the various ways in which the Mass has been celebrated for centuries. As early as 1671 a history of the Mass by Cardinal Bona was published, and nine years later the learned Italian Cardinal Giuseppe-Maria Tommasi published a study of early Roman and Gallican liturgies. Interest in Eastern liturgies grew and an appreciation of their relevance to Western practices was acknowledged by scholars. For example, in the Byzantine rite, immediately after the consecration the celebrant chants: "We offer you your own, from what is your own, in all and for the sake of all."

By the 19th century an awareness of the importance of an understanding of the ceremonies and prayers of the Mass for complete participation of those attending, laity as well as clerics, began a movement which was to grow during the next hundred years, until it culminated in the revised liturgy of Vatican II. Dom Prosper Gueranger, Abbot of Solesmes, the Benedictine Abbey that became famous for the Gregorian chant, may properly be called the founder of this renewal, although some critics feel that monasteries themselves tended to produce a liturgy far removed from the capabilities and needs of the ordinary layman in the parish church. However, there is no question that the Benedictines loved the liturgy and promoted devotional performance of the Mass, and through homilies carefully prepared for the congregation brought about a more spiritual and authentic understanding of the service. Influential names are numerous, the most important, perhaps, being Dom Lambert Beauduin.

In France the Gallican liturgical movement disturbed the Congregation of Rites in Rome. It is amusing to note that Father Jube, parish priest of Asnières, near Paris, was a special target of their concern. It is amusing, because much of what he was experimenting with was incorporated a century later into Vatican II's *Constitution on the Sacred Liturgy*. For example: he never used the high altar except on Sundays and major feasts when he had a large congregation. The altar had no lights or cross except the processional cross and candles carried in, and placed on the altar at the beginning of Mass. His congregation was encouraged to become involved in the preparation, the psalm and confession and absolution. After he had sung the collect he sat down and listened to other ministers, sometimes members of the congregation, read the epistle and gospel. His offertory procession included offerings of all kinds, was brought up from the body of the church by the laity. He never began the canon before the choir had finished the *Sanctus* and *Benedictus*, and his prayers were always said distinctly so that the congregation might hear and comprehend. Obviously, like the Gallican liturgists, he was an innovater in the sense that to him, the authority for the liturgy was neither Medieval nor Tridentine, but the early Church.

Most Americans, even today, are unaware of the very early involvement our own leaders had in the effort to "return the Mass to the people." The first proponent of liturgical reform was the father of the American hierarchy, Archbishop John Carroll. He had views and ideas about bringing the people closer to the official channels of God's life, that as Father Paul Marx notes, "make some attitudes today very conservative by comparison." As early as 1789 he was urging the use of the vernacular, and as John Tracy Ellis pointed out, Carroll would have been in the vanguard of any movement to bring the sublime offices of the Church closer to the faithful by having as much as possible of the liturgical service performed in a language which they fully understood. John England, first Bishop of Charleston edited a missal for the laity in English which was published in 1822, and almost got Bishop England in trouble with the Holy See.

An address to a Catholic conference in Malines, Belgium, in 1909 by the Benedictine, Dom Lambert, accelerated the movement of involving the whole people of God in the celebration of Mass. Almost immediately after the address, weekly sheets on the texts of the Sunday Mass were prepared for use in parishes, sheets which were bound, and resembled today's Missalettes. How revolutionary this was is difficult for today's Catholic to realize, but as late as 1857 the prayers of the Mass were not to be translated for the use of the people, Pope Pius IX, renewing an earlier prohibition in that year. It was not until 1898 that translations of the missal were no longer censured and put on the *Index of Forbidden Books*. From 1920 on, the missals of Dom Lefebvre made the long untranslated Mass prayers available to people in their own language, thus permitting them to participate in a new way.

In the United States, in this century, the center of liturgical renewal was the Benedictine Abbey of St. John, Collegeville, Minnesota, which in the twenties began to publish the magazine *Orate, Fratres,* now called *Worship.* So daring was this, that in a few seminaries where courses in liturgy meant rubrics, the magazine was at first forbidden reading. Its founder and first editor was Father

THE MASS

Virgil Michel, and its contributors, then and now, included some of the most influential scholars in America: Godfrey Diekmann, Michel's confrere, Joseph Busch, Bishop of St. Cloud, and Austin Dowling, Archbishop of St. Paul. Liturgical scholars who were pastors, such as H. A. Reinhold and Martin Hellriegel, brought the seeds of renewal to parish liturgies, and scholars such as Gerard Ellard, S.J., and William Puetter, S.J., were faithful researchers and writers of liturgical books. Another Jesuit, Daniel Lord, deserves credit for interesting the young in the liturgy through his Summer Schools of Catholic Action, at which he introduced sodalists and their teachers to the dialogue Mass, which as far back as 1947 had been encouraged by Pius XII in *Mediator Dei*, the first encyclical in the history of the Church to be devoted entirely to the liturgy.

These early liturgists often found that their endeavors were sometimes looked upon as a "midwestern fad," an attitude that characterized the annual National Liturgical Week as "a meeting of a bunch of Germans out in the Midwest." There was some justification for the ethnic epithet, since German-American priests, such as Bede Maler, a monk of St. Meinrad's Abbey, saw the need of a liturgical movement as early as 1891, long before Dom Virgil Michel came on the scene.

In a letter to Father Michel's Abbot, Maler, by

then an old man, urged the Abbot to encourage the young Michel, since, as he said, "I am old and miserable, and not able to do anything but nag and criticize. . . . I will rejoice with all my heart when . . . our people are given strong food and not this sentimental sugar-bread of awful, lovely devotions."

One who tried to do just that was Martin Carrabine, S.J., who, through weekly meetings of CISCA, made Chicago high school and college students aware both of the implications of the Mass, and the social obligations implied. At these weekly meetings young people were imbued with the realization that the Mass is the chief act of divine worship, and should also be the source and center of Christian piety. At the same time Father Carrabine launched his young friends into exciting discussions of the liturgy as eminently social, leading them to discover for themselves the need to live daily what they celebrated at Mass. Those who heard him protest unchristian individualism and subjectivism in religion would never forget his insistence that to go that road inevitably led to spiritual and social selfishness.

The dialogue Mass, or as it was known in the first decade of its popularity in the United States, as *Missa Recitata*, through its use in high schools and colleges, soon became an ordinary part of the American Mass. Its acceptance was a surprise even to those who risked publishing the first daily Missal in this century, the Lohmann Company of St. Paul. Archbishop Dowling, ordinarily a supporter of the whole liturgical movement wrote, "A missal is a fine book for a priest or a nun, but it is expecting just too much from the laity to have them use a missal."

The Archbishop was wrong, as Archbishops sometimes are, and in its first year the publisher sold 4,826 copies. By 1952 Lohmann reported several million copies had been sold. Kenedy, which jumped on the band-wagon, reported a yearly average of 4,000 missals from 1924-28, by which time over 50,000 copies had been sold. Even with today's use of the Missalette in most churches, daily missals are still sold for the hearing-impaired. The laity were not only ready for participation in the Mass; they were hungry for it. Out of that closer involvement in the Eucharistic life of the Church was to come a more open response to the social character it implied, and responsibilities of participants to become actively engaged in social awareness.

As C. J. Mc Naspy, S.J., pointed out in his introduction to the *Constitution on the Sacred Liturgy* in Walter Abbott's translation of the *Documents of Vatican II*, the astonishing growth of interest in the liturgy indicates that this was no passing phenomenon, and the vast research and studies of scholars made it possible for a series of reforms to be undertaken in line with the Church's deepest traditions. All the basic groundwork had been done.

Some changes in liturgical practices had already slipped by for special circumstances: in 1929 permission was given (but not published) authorizing the celebration of the Eucharist in the afternoon and evening in Russia, on condition that a Eucharistic fast of four hours from noon be observed. Military chaplains were allowed to celebrate evening Masses from 1940. The generalizing of these concessions in 1957 to make it possible for working people to attend Mass more frequently also brought about the reduction of the fast to an hour in 1964.

The restoration of the Easter Vigil to its ancient place on Holy Saturday night in 1951, on an experimental basis, pointed to things to come. The Congregation of Rites observed that priests had been led to believe that a revision of the Breviary and Missal was imminent, but added in *Osservatore Romano,* May 4, 1955, that "such a revision will require several years." What is hidden in that bland statement is the denial that the change was even then being contemplated.

The *Constitution on the Sacred Liturgy,* the first document considered at Vatican II, was submitted to much discussion, to debates (328 interruptions!) and final revision. On November 14, 2,162 Council Fathers voted in favor of the schema with only 46 negative votes. Amendments were studied and when possible, incorporated into the final text, and at the concluding vote there were 2,147 in favor and only 4 against. Pope Paul VI promulgated it on December 4, 1963. As Roger Marchand commented, "It was the end of an age."

Originally this was the point at which this chapter was to end, but after a superficial survey of some of my friends, a survey so casual it would certainly not receive the approval of NORC or any other professional group of statisticians, I decided I had taken too much for granted. The questions I put to about twenty-five or thirty friends, all of whom are intelligent, well-educated, and dedicated Catholics, brought surprising answers. The questions were: 1) Have you read *The Constitution on the Liturgy?* and 2) Can you tell me at least four things it says?

The answers were interesting. A number admitted they had not read the document but had read about it or heard it explained (more or less) in homilies. Several of those who said they had read it admitted it was too long ago to expect them to remember any specific recommendations. The answers to the second question from those who essayed it were amusing. One stated that the *Alleluia* was always to be sung; another thought the *Sanctus* carried the same recommendation. One recalled, or thought she did, that the 30-second interval between the reading of the Epistle and the Responsorial hymn was so that the faithful might meditate on the Epistle. Another claimed reading some footnote that permitted the congregation to gather around the altar after the Offertory as a decision of the Council Fathers. Another, who claimed she had attended a liturgical workshop on the Constitution, insisted she had been told that although women could serve as extraordinary ministers in bringing Communion to the sick, they could not enter the sanctuary to get the hosts. Another woman who had attended the same meeting recalled being told that while they could on certain unspecified occasions assist in distributing Communion during the Mass, neither they nor their small daughters could serve as acolytes, since they were not permitted to touch the Missal. One interviewee, to my astonishment, had not only read the document, and remembered it, but could actually quote whole sections. She admitted, a bit sheepishly, that she taught it in a course on the Council. Actually, few of these memories appear in the Constitution, although some have become the norm in a number of parishes, an outgrowth of the recommendations and authority given Bishops to approve certain cultural rites which seem to serve their dioceses.

As a result of this totally unscientific survey I decided to include something of the proceedings of the Council that produced this particular document, but also to summarize Part II, the section on the Mass, followed by a bit of relevant material on the Commission authorized by the Council to draw up for implementation some of the more universal rites. It is important to remember, however, that the *Constitution on the Liturgy,* as the Benedictine liturgist, Salvatore Marsili reminded the readers of *L'Osservatore Romano,* was not only a code of rubrics, but called for a reformation of mind and mentality in ceremonial matters based on new theological perspectives.

Indeed as Xavier Rynne summarized in his book, *Second Session,* the Constitution established the function of the Word of God in liturgical worship, placing the emphasis on Scripture as understood in and by modern biblical theology; thereby furnishing a realistic bridge for a dialogue with the Protestant churches, whose worship has always been biblically rather than sacramentally oriented. This, of course, correlates with a later Conciliar document on ecumenism, a fact that underscores the concern the Council Fathers had that, as far as possible, all the documents should indicate a uniform thrust, not only for the members of the Church, but for all the children of God.

The Constitution also established the need and right for greater participation by the people in church worship, and the duty of episcopal conferences to spell out the practical details of adapting the Church's worship to local conditions. According to Rynne, this last provision was an important preliminary step in acknowledging the collegial character of the bishops, as acknowledgment which broke the tight control which the Roman Congregation of Rites had exercised for many years.

What makes the Eucharistic declaration of Vatican II significantly different from some earlier Councils in which the Mass was discussed, and regulations for its celebration drawn up, is that in the Vatican II debates, acrimonious as they occasionally became, the central matter of the Mass was always the subject. That Christ was present, whole and entire in both bread and wine was simply taken for granted. Quibbling over terms such as transubstantiation, oral manducation was simply brushed aside; the moment at which Christ became present was not matter for argument. That the Mass is both sacrifice and sacrament was agreed upon, and the term Eucharistic meal had few opponents, although the passion, death and resurrection as a part of that memorial meal were never forgotten. The more complete participation of the laity was not a controversial element; all the Council Fathers agreed that by virtue of their Baptism, the people of God offer the Eucharist with the celebrant, and join with him in the reception of the Body and Blood of Christ, through whose divine energy they would be enabled to make a sacrificial offering of their lives to God and their neighbor in their work. As liturgists throughout the world had been insisting, the giving of self at Mass will always be a sham unless it includes the pledge of serving neighbor in God. This emphasis, obviously, stresses the corporate social order of the Mass.

Today, more than twenty years later, the reports of the sessions during which the Constitution was under discussion seem to be problems of another age, as indeed, they are. The real hurdle during the first session had to do with the use of the vernacular in Mass, and the other sacraments, in place of Latin, and should such "local option" be allowed, who would make the decisions: the local Ordinary who knew his culture and his people, or the Congregation of Rites which had been in control for centuries? Liturgists in the Western world had acquainted their Bishops with the advantages of the use of a language that participants in the liturgy understood, even though some Western Bishops, including at least two strong voices from the United States, were vocal proponents of retaining Latin. It was the voices from prelates active in Asia, Africa, South America, and those already using non-Latin rites, who spoke most convincingly from their own experience in attempting to adapt the Church's prayers and ceremonials to cultures whose differing preoccupations, and social and economic needs were at opposite poles from those who had formulated the liturgy. Maximos IV Saigh, Melchite Patriarch of Antioch (who spoke in French because, as he said, Latin was not the language of the Eastern church) gave one of the more impressive discussions on the subject of vernacular in the Mass. "Christ, after all, talked in the language of his contemporaries, and it was also in Aramaic that he offered the first sacrifice of the Eucharist, in a language understood by all the people who heard him. The Apostles and Disciples did the same. It would never have occurred to them that, in a Christian assembly, the celebrant should deliver the scriptural lessons, or sing the psalms, or preach or break bread in a language other than that of the gathered faithful." Then he added, "Every language is, in effect, liturgical, for following the advice of the psalmist, *Laudate Dominum, omnes gentes*, it is proper to glorify God, preach the Gospel and offer the sacrifice in any language whatsoever."

Interestingly enough, it was the Curial Father, Cardinal Tisserant, who called the Council's attention to the fact that Slavic languages as well as Chinese had been recognized by the Congregation of Rites as permissible liturgical languages. Cardinal Gracias of Madras, India, added that from his own background he felt vernacular languages were absolutely necessary for ordinary people, and that the question should be left to the decision of conferences of bishops. Bishop Descuffi of Smyrna reminded the prelates that as Christ had said earlier about the law—the liturgy, too, was for the benefit of man and not man for the liturgy. He also noted that to make special arrangements for missionary countries was ludicrous, since today every country is a missionary country.

The proponents of the use of the vernacular won, as we know, as did the right of the local Bishops' Conferences to decide on what would be most appropriate in their own dioceses.

The recommendations of the Commission did not end there, but nothing else resulted in such debate nor took so long to decide. Even the more important shift of language in the emphasis of the Mass from sacrifice to sacrifice and sacrament, with the division breaking into the celebration of the Word and that of the Eucharist as distinct from the earlier "essential parts"—Offertory, Consecration, and Communion—were agreed upon with little difficulty.

Aside from this use of the vernacular, what did the *Constitution for the Restoration and Promotion of the Sacred Liturgy* give us regarding the Eucharist? Actually nothing doctrinal: recognition of the Way, the Truth and the Life, Christ Jesus, was already there in the Bread and Wine. But the change of emphasis was significant, and the open-ended possibilities for the ritual surrounding the celebration of Mass will affect ages yet unborn. To be a bit more specific: this book touches only on Chapter 2 of the Constitution, which deals with the general norms for the celebration of the Eucharist, not with the chapters covering the liturgical life in dioceses and parishes, or with the other sacraments and sacramentals, the Divine Office, Music, Art, furnishings for the altar, vestments or the liturgical year, except for those Articles which relate specifically to the Mass.

Jungmann, a member of the Commission that wrote the Constitution, in a Commentary on the Documents of Vatican II expresses the mind of the Council Fathers when he points out that public worship is the point at which the mystery of Christ continues to operate. It is the heart of a Christian's ecclesial and personal life. Topics resulting from the modern technological world could not be ignored. For example, the question whether broadcasting and televising of the Mass was in keeping with its dignity was occasion for a long and lively controversy. Amusingly enough, the whole question was redundant, since the practice of televising Papal Masses in St. Peter's had already become a tradition.

There was almost unanimous insistence that the Eucharist should be celebrated in such a way that it is closely connected with the life and feelings of the people. "Noble simplicity" is the word the Commis-

THE MASS

sion uses. While noting that the Eucharist is for the glorification of God, Article 33 maintains that it should also be a school of faith, not only in the lessons and homilies, but in its prayers, its signs and symbols—a side neglected in the last centuries.

In a broad sense the whole work of the liturgical reform was one of adaptation to changed times. The global village of the 20th century demanded an affirmation of the indigenous values of other cultures. As a result, a certain elasticity of written norms became characteristic of the renewed liturgy. The Body of Christ had to be brought back into oneness with the Body of Christ in the pew, as one liturgist put it. Our preoccupation with the transubstantiation of the bread had to be placed in the context of the transformation of the congregation. To say that the individual members of the assembly are so united in the risen Lord that he and they are Christ now, may seem new or even radical to some. But already in the 4th century St. Augustine was reminding his people, "If then you are the body of Christ and his members, it is your sacrament that reposes on the altar of the Lord. Be what you see, and receive what you are. There you are on the table, and there you are in the chalice."

A startling statement this, and as John Haughey warns, "Eucharist is dangerous food to eat because it makes its consumers what they eat. And what they eat died on a cross." Perilous business indeed!

Mary Hester Valentine

Article 48 reiterates the principle that the faithful are to be nourished both at the table of the Word and the table of the sacrament. They are called to active participation, and the reintroduction of the ancient tradition of prayer after the homily underscores this in a specific way. While allowing for personal and local needs, the formula of these bidding prayers should always include the great perpetual concerns of the Church and mankind.

Communion is given under both species when feasible, a decision reached only after considerable heated debate. Those opposed cited hygienic problems, and one Cardinal reported that women with lipstick regularly approached the altar for communion. Those in favor reminded the Council Fathers that the words of Christ were, "If you do not eat the flesh of the Son of man and drink his blood . . ." (*John* 6:53) and that argument was incontrovertible. It was further recommended that the Communion by the faithful be of the elements consecrated during the same Mass.

It is clear that this active, corporate participation aimed to become an antidote to the deadening formalism and routine in set forms of worship.

Inevitably there have been problems in the implementing of these significant changes, and some were foreseen by the Council Fathers. As George Every notes in discussing the adaptations to the great variety of cultural circumstances, there were

THE MASS

fears that the introduction of elements from the traditions and cultures of some countries, for instance, the ritual dances in Africa and Indonesia, would lead to developments and rites which could be interpreted by psychoanalysts, anthropologists and Evangelical missionaries in an erotic and sinister sense. But Bishop Van Bekkum of Ruteng in Indonesia, speaking to this point, said that the current rites then in use could be freed from the suspicion that they were magical only if they were performed in the context of a particular cultural situation. African Bishops agreed with him whole-heartedly, and as a result, the diversity of approved rites stood.

Kevin Seasoltz in his study of the preconciliar commission, emphasizes that that body dealt with four points: the desire and need for vernacular in the liturgy, the pastoral character of the liturgy, the need for cultural adaptation for all countries, and a desire for concelebration. This last point went through an involved debate before being accepted, and Father Mc Naspy, commenting on its use, at least in the United States, feels that it was introduced all too quickly, and that the homework had not been adequately done. As a result, it does not appear to have achieved what it was intended: a form of Eucharist by which the unity of the priesthood is appropriately manifested. Seasoltz seems to agree with Mc Naspy by pointing out that the ritual seems to be more a gesture of self-affirmation on the part of the priests concelebration than an affirmation of their unitive role in the community. The ritual becomes primatial rather than a ministerial symbol. But current problems with this, as with other parts of the liturgical renewal which have been cause for controversy, will be discussed in the next chapter of this book.

Before moving on, however, I should like to point out that Seaholtz speaks for many when he indicates that the decision to maintain the creed in its traditional position between the homily and the prayer of the faithful is looked upon as a structural flaw. The homily is meant to mediate the Word of the Lord to the assembled community, and to stir up a response of faith and trust, which is reflected in the prayer of the faithful. But when the creed is interjected between the homily and the prayer of the faithful, it fractures the unity of the rite.

He also notes that liturgists also object to the offertory prayers, which they feel, complicate what should be a very simple preparation of the gifts. But many find these prayers some of the finest in the new liturgy and object to music during their recitation, especially since they call for response from the faithful.

Summarizing what was actually accomplished, rather than getting into the complex issues of contemporary thinking, opposition and debate, seems to be called for here. The most evident achievement is the shift of emphasis from the Eucharist from sacrifice only to the earlier patristic belief in the Eucharistic celebration as both sacrament and sacrifice. The renewal and restoration of purified ancient rites allied with a recognition of the fact that uniformity in liturgy did not necessarily imply unity, allows for cultural diversity, a recognition of respect which grew out of the pastoral orientation of the Council. The core of the Church's official teaching on the liturgy is stressed in Article 10, . . . "the liturgy is the fountain from which all her power (the Church) flows. For the goal of all apostolic works is that all who are made sons of God by faith and baptism should come together to praise God in the midst of his Church, to take part in her sacrifice, and to eat the Lord's supper." Everything in the Constitution, all changes in liturgy have, therefore, as their end, the active, fruitful participation of the faithful so that "the life of Jesus may be visible in our mortal flesh" (2 Cor. 4:10-11).

The changes in the prayers said during the Mass, while extremely important to the theologians and liturgists who made them, have been less obvious to the majority of the faithful, and reasons for the changes, important though they are in the context of the celebration, have seldom been explained. As a result, many are unaware that the new missal was following the recommendations of the Council, which decided that in order to achieve the desired end: the adaptation to the needs of our times, full and active participation by the laity was to be encouraged.

The word *revised* is repeated twenty times in the *Constitution on the Liturgy.*

Pierre Loret points out that as early as 1964 Pope Paul VI had set up a commission of international liturgical experts including cardinals, bishops, and pastors of parishes. The new Roman Missal appeared on March 26, 1970, and a revised edition with minor changes came out in 1975. In the new missal the greeting is preceded by the Sign of the Cross, to which the people answer *Amen.* Robert Cabie points out that the greeting and response are no longer the first words exchanged by priest and congregation, an alteration he calls regrettable. In many parishes the celebrant precedes the formal opening of the service with a greeting, "Good morning," or "Good evening," as the case may be.

In addition to the readings usually borrowed from the *Acts* and letters of the Apostles, provision is now made for a third reading for Sundays and feast days, this time from the Old Testament, which must always be selected for its relation to the Gospel of the day, although to the ordinary layman in the pew this relationship sometimes seems farfetched. The passages in the Synoptic Gospels are proclaimed in a three-year cycle on the Sundays of

THE MASS

Ordinary time: Matthew in year A, Mark in year B, and Luke in year C. In special seasons, particularly during Lent until Pentecost, the Gospel of John is proclaimed. There is no obvious link between the readings of the Old Testament from Sunday to Sunday, a decision made to emphasize the fact that the gospel is the fulfillment of the prophecies and the promises made to Israel.

Basil Pennington, commenting on the reading of the Gospel, points out that when it is read at the Mass, Jesus again proclaims his good news, speaking now to us as he spoke to the crowds in Galilee. Because in our culture it is appropriate to stand at attention during an especially significant moment, we stand for this reading.

Mary Durkin in *The Eucharist,* summarizes the simplifying of the rites by stating that those "extraneous features that were added over time or were duplicated were eliminated, especially those having to do with the preparation of the bread and wine, the Breaking of the Bread, and the Communion." The Offertory prayers that were repetitious and intruded on the Eucharistic prayer were eliminated, the result being not only shorter, but modeled on the prayer of the Jewish father at a ritual meal.

Just recently I gave a copy of the Easter season Missalette to a Jewish friend who, for years, has been giving our convent "kosher" matzos, bitter

Mary Hester Valentine

herbs, wine, and other prescribed foods for our Holy Thursday Passover meal. She wrote me shortly after to say she found our service "interesting, for it so resembles seder." I was gratified that my friend recognized the similarity.

The previously untouchable Canon was remodeled, although the oriental liturgies have always had variety in the anaphoras (the prayers expressing the sacred offering.) Pope Paul VI in the *Apostolic Constitution* of April 3, 1969, reported on the new Eucharistic prayer with its more than 80 Prefaces, "some drawn from the more ancient traditions of the Roman Church, and some newly composed." The Pope himself added three more Canons, with the admonition that "for pastoral reasons, and so to facilitate concelebration, we have ordered that the words of our Lord shall be the same in all forms of the Canon. In every Eucharistic prayer, therefore, we wish these words to read as follows: Over the bread: TAKE THIS, ALL OF YOU, AND EAT IT: THIS IS MY BODY WHICH WILL BE GIVEN UP FOR YOU. Over the wine: TAKE THIS, ALL OF YOU, AND DRINK FROM IT: THIS IS THE CUP OF MY BLOOD, THE BLOOD OF THE NEW AND EVERLASTING COVENANT. IT WILL BE SHED FOR YOU AND FOR ALL SO THAT SINS MAY BE FORGIVEN. DO THIS IN MEMORY OF ME."

THE MASS

Three Eucharistic prayers have been added. The first is an adaptation of the anaphora of Hippolytus of Rome. The second of the new prayers is a revised version composed by the Commission as an alternative to the Roman Canon. The last prayer is based on the structures found in Eastern anaphoras, such as that of St. Basil.

A feature of the early Roman rite, the kiss of peace immediately before Communion, was revived. Tertullian noted that this kiss of peace was looked upon as the seal put upon the prayer. After the 13th century a peculiar adaptation of the practice was introduced in England. A "kissing board," or *Pax* board was passed around: each one received the board, kissed it, and passed it on. The recommendation for the kiss of peace today, according to Cabie, is that it "is to be adapted to the possible sensibilities of various cultures." In the United States in large parish groups a hand shake has become the custom; in closer-knit groups—friends or family, the embrace may be warm and familiar. I have witnessed, and been moved by seeing, even in large parishes, married couples smile at each other and then embrace, then turn to their children and give them the same warm assurance of their Christian human bond.

This gesture, whether the more formalized handshake of good will, or the more intimate loving embrace is a manifestation of Christ's prayer for us, "That you all may be one, as I and my Father are one." Father Bernard Lee underscores the intention of the Council that the Eucharist be the primary way by which Christian unity is both signified and brought about. The unity is not to be something abstract or mystical, but concrete, social, evident and verifiable. The sign of this unity is not the Eucharist as such, but the community brought about by the Eucharist. To be that sign of unity there has to be a Community of human beings whose relationship with one another is such that the neutral observer can see and know they are Christians in their love, united in the body of Christ.

John J. Egan, speaking at a liturgical meeting on the unfinished agenda of the Liturgy, urged his listeners to reemphasize the heritage that insists that by drawing together around the altar as one people, united with one another in Christ, reaching out to all others in love and service in order to draw all to share in the life of unity and love which God intends for them. That is what Eucharist is all about.

CONTEMPORARY THINKING
AND DEBATE

SINCE THE *Constitution on the Sacred Liturgy* had as one of its primary aims the involvement of the faithful in the celebration of the Mass, and since the document was the result, not only of the serious thinking and debate on the part of the Council Fathers during Vatican II, but also of the months and years of preparation by liturgists and theologians, it seems strange that its implementation has been not only slow but divisive. There are, of course, several reasons for this. Anyone who has been a member of a task force for a project involving change, or a member of a committee charged with studying some plan to be adopted by a group or organization knows the frustration attendant upon the reaction to the proposal. A simple recognition of the fact that what is being presented to the group comes to them cold, with none of the hours of debate and argument evident, would alleviate some of the difficulty for the presentors. Problems raised have been dealt with in committee, sometimes exhaustively and acrimoniously, but none of this appears to those reading the document for the first time.

It was not that the Council Fathers did not realize the gap which would remain between the promulgation of the document and its recipients. Pierre Lorel, commenting on this aspect of the work, notes that during the deliberations experts were polishing their work, Bishops were issuing directives, the Pope was pondering, and translators were sharpening their pencils. In short, everybody involved was thinking in terms of history. But meanwhile, what about preparing the people for changes that would shatter a liturgical mold that was centuries old?

Kevin Seasoltz, commenting on the Conciliar Fathers' awareness of this problem, points out that the implementation of the new rites was to be accompanied by liturgical catechesis: bishops and pastors were charged with the preparation of doctrinal background for the proposed changes. Liturgists have been pointing out for the more than quarter of a century since the Constitution was approved, that much work still remains to be done. Theoretically, the reform of the liturgy should be virtually complete. Although the problems that the contemporary world and its varied cultures raise were pointed out clearly by the Council, together with the principles to be followed in solving them, the application of these principles, as Robert Cabie pointed out, led to a revision of perspectives and decisions which could not have been anticipated in 1965.

As a result, liturgical reform often became a source of division, and the cause of considerable anguish and confusion. It would be easy to blame this on the reluctance of pastors to instruct parishioners on the thinking behind the changes, but in many cases, the pastors themselves were not fully cognizant of the rationale, since they had not been present at the discussions and studies out of which the renewal emerged. There were, of course, some priests who simply announced that as of a certain date Mass would be said in English, the altar would be turned so that the priest would face the congregation, the altar rail would be removed, and people would stand to receive Communion, which might be received in the hand, and all this "because Rome wants it that way."

John Egan emphasizes that the importance of liturgical reform for the renewal of church life is acknowledged in the opening paragraph of the Constitution, and yet the document never suggests any way to overcome the problem of the connection between liturgy and the social life of the faithful.

As Egan and many others see it, initially, liturgical reform was expected to revitalize the communal life of the church. If liturgy was the public communal worship, then it seemed that a liturgy marked by vernacular language, greater congregational participation, and adaptation to the needs and concerns of particular groups would bring about an intensification of community, a deeper faith, and a more active sense of mission. But it did not work out quite that smoothly.

People cling to many things merely because they have been handed down, as though through long usage in the religious sphere they had received a special kind of consecration, had become sacralized, holy. As such they are in stark contrast to the simplicity and interiority we encounter in the writings of the New Testament.

Another source of division was the lack of clarity regarding the new emphasis on the Church community. Some socially minded pastors began to emphasize the renewal of community life, believing that the new sense of community would find expression in the liturgy. But as John Egan questioned, "Do you renew community to create good liturgy, or reform the liturgy to create community?" In some areas of the Church, the texts themselves have been perceived as sterile directives, subject to no subtlety or ambiguity and allowing no measure of nuanced interpretation. Frequently enough the translations themselves are atrocious, about which more will be said later.

And then, of course, there have been vast cultural developments taking place throughout the world, not only in the so-called third world, but also in the highly developed technological countries. The confusion engendered had multiple causes, and not all have been addressed even now. I will deal with some of these in this chapter, and in the final chapter, changes which may be presumed, with reservations, of course, as anything dealing with the future must be.

Bishop Gaughan is not the only one who has noted that it would appear that more Catholics are missing Sunday Mass now than at the time of Vatican II. Isais Powers, C.P., states that in 1960, 83% of Catholics went to Mass every Sunday; in 1988 only 31% were going. In his book, *Troubled Catholics*, Bishop Gaughan remarks that percentages vary, but the implications behind them is that this demands immediate attention if not remedy. A balanced observer, Bishop Gaughan questions whether there may not be fewer Catholics, and whether, in fact, the Catholic population has been affected by the fluctuation of the birth rate in the United States in the past 25 years.

Another of his wise comments on the reports on dropouts is that perhaps there are people "who would not buy a committee-decided liturgy, a process arrived at, a set of rules called 'renewal' paraliturgical rites which were aimed at the lowest common denominator, and did not create room or make allowances for those who wanted to be different."

It is some of these issues with which this chapter will deal. The rubrical provisions pertaining exclusively to the celebrant I will leave to those in a better position to evaluate the theological reasoning behind the optional variants left to the judgment of the celebrants: the number of genuflections, the number of crosses to be made over the offerings, the type of vestments to be worn. This chapter will concentrate on areas of the reform which apply more directly to the laity and about which they grumble the most, chiefly because they are not sure what the new liturgy hoped to accomplish.

As has been pointed out earlier, the changes were prompted by the new awareness of ancient historical origins, the discovery of old liturgies, the developing study of comparative liturgies, and a renewed focus on the Mass as the assembly of the faithful, who themselves actively offer the sacrifice with the priest, as Pope Pius XII insisted in his encyclical *Mediator Dei* in 1947.

Probably one of the reasons criticism has focused on minor issues is that theological debate has been comparatively limited. Perhaps the most important issue was that Mary Durkin noted in *The Eucharist*, the joining together of the theology of the Eucharist and the theology of the liturgy, a unity which comes from the understanding of the Eucharist as sacramental action rather than just sacramental object. She calls attention to "those interpretations that emphasize the Eucharist as sacrifice, as Real Presence, and as cause of unity. Theologians see the Eucharist as meal, memorial, thanksgiving, eschatological challenge, justification, and impetus to social action, all of which have roots in both Scripture and tradition. Vatican II did not explicitly spell out a definition, but specifies that "in the most blessed Eucharist is contained the whole spiritual good of the Church, Christ himself, our Pasch, and the living bread which gives life to men."

The emphasis on "the table of the Word," according to Stenzel stems from the language of the Fathers, and raises the Word of God "to the dignity of that from which the congregation can live." So, what both the celebrant and the faithful bring to the Eucharist is an awareness of unchanging faith and unbroken tradition, a tradition which expresses that faith with varying emphases as centuries pass.

It is to Cardinal Bea that we owe the emphasis on Scripture reading and the homily, for the original text of the schema had only required that the faithful should "understand the rites and prayers well." Cardinal Bea emphasized that this was not adequate, and that the faithful should rather understand the mystery itself through the prayers and rites, clearly a justifiable demand. The faithful are to be nourished at the double table: the table of the Word and the table of the sacrament.

The Offertory procession is no longer a novelty; the symbolism of placing the gifts upon the altar has been clarified, and the Offertory of the faithful is recognized as an integral part of the Eucharist in which celebrant and people both participate. Current practice also includes on special occasions more than the bread and wine. Symbolic items, such as banners, and "tools of the trade" in commemorative Masses: books, work boxes, sheet music, or an instrument, memorialize the emphasis on contributed service.

In one Milwaukee church I have attended, in addition to the formal Offertory procession and the usual collection by the ushers (during which the celebrant sits instead of continuing the Mass as he might have done in a pre-conciliar service, which elevated the importance of the collection above the celebration of the Mass), there is an informal, anonymous third collection. Along one side of the church a long table stands, and as parishioners come in for their weekly Sunday Mass they put packages and bags of food, or clothing, for distribution to the centers which serve the needy of the city, on this table. I understand this parish also seeks out its own poor, ill or incapacitated and elderly members, and visits them on a regular basis to offer help as needed. It is their 20th century recognition that the Mass is a sacrament of unity, and if it does not result in direct action, participants are playing a pious game.

At a time when our documents on social justice are stronger than ever we need to be reminded that words and committees do not change the world, and that as Pedro Arrupe said at the International

THE MASS

Eucharistic Congress in Philadelphia in 1974, "If there is hunger anywhere in the world, then our celebration of the Eucharist is somehow, everywhere incomplete in the world. He comes to us not alone, but with the poor, the oppressed, the starving of the earth. Through him they are looking for help, for justice, for love expressed in action. We cannot properly receive the Bread of Life unless at the same time we give bread for life to those in need, wherever, whoever they may be." Christ is the motive, the source, the guarantee of this urgently needed change, but it will not come about if, as John Egan said, "We have taken the agenda of Vatican II as a call to hold hands in the liturgy and share coffee with our own kind afterwards."

Henri de Lubac emphasizes that unity is realized in the Church, since the Church creates the Eucharist, but the Eucharist also creates the Church. This was one of the obvious reasons for restoring communion under both species. All of us eat of the flesh of the Son of Man, and drink his blood, and thus share his life in each other. Note, the permission for reception of both species is not an obligation, and those of the faithful who are germ-conscious can pass up the ciborium/chalice. Obviously, then, this change should not be cause for distress, but there are those who continue to stress the dangers of infection. There are also those who for the same reason fret about receiving communion in the hand, preferring to open their mouths like little birds in the nest being fed. Their problem: the hand has been shown to be the major carrier of infectious diseases; surprisingly they do not consider the priest's hand, which distributes the host, a risk. Obviously, the frail, the sick, the trembling have quite another reason for not receiving in the hand.

Which brings us to the contemporary emphasis on the Eucharist as meal. Jungmann points out that even though the meal is not the basic form of the Mass as a whole, it is still an indispensable and essential part of it. Communion is the sacrificial banquet; the people's Communion is the fulfillment of Christ's desire to draw his own unto himself, and to take them with him to his Father, but it also demands on their part sacramental self-abandonment to his sacrificial self-surrender. As St. John Chrysostom sees in the hand that presents the consecrated Host the outstretched hand of the Lord himself, so must we.

Cabie reminds us that reception of the bread suggests a nourishment for a journey, and fellowship at the same table. Reception of the cup conjures up a feast that gives a foretaste of the banquet in the kingdom.

It is Basil Pennington who warns that it must always be clear that the Eucharist is a memorial of Christ's paschal mystery, and we should be aware of a danger of centering the liturgy too much on everyday life, of reducing it to a celebration of the human—social, political, even revolutionary. The Eucharist and human life, he notes, should form one fabric, but in the weaving, the mystery should not be reduced. For while in earlier times, when the reception of Communion was a rarity, and the celebration of the sacrifice tended to obscure the meal, today there is danger that the celebration of the meal may obscure the sacrifice, especially in informal Eucharists.

Unity is the heart and center of the Eucharist. But we have such power to frustrate the most sublime and beautiful designs of the Almighty that Communion itself has been turned into an occasion of discord and disunity. As an example of this sort of divisive tactic, the *National Catholic Reporter* of May 18, 1990 carried the news story that Bishop Donald Montrose of Stockton, California, in an open letter to priests in the diocesan paper, *Catholic Lantern*, ordered parishes to put an end to row by row reception of communion, because it encourages people to receive communion who should not. Father Francis Larry Dunphy's problem is people who are not going to communion who could. *NCR* commented that Bishop Montrose clearly wants to emphasize the idea of sacrificing, the idea of the ordained priesthood, and in this theology he has not included much treatment of Eucharist as meal or as family celebration.

Mary Hester Valentine

The Eucharist is constituted of bread and wine, both of which are clearly meant to be eaten and drunk, and Raymond Brown emphasizes that communion is of the very essence of the Eucharistic celebration. The performance of what Christ has instituted would not be complete without communion. Brown's comments include a *caveat* as he warns that recently, Jesus' action of presenting the species as food and drink is given so much prominence, that upon superficial consideration one could be tempted to read into the action nothing more than a meal, and thus to reduce the Institution to a mere ritual. He points out that the same temptations seem to hold an attraction for Catholics keen on ecumenical dialogue, and witnesses the tendency not only to take over from the Reformed churches the expression supper or banquet as a possible synecdoche, but further, to adopt the concept itself as adequately describing the whole reality.

It is Bishop Gaughan, again, who questions this aspect of our celebrating the Eucharist, when he asks if the sense of decline in reverence towards the Eucharist is brought about in part by the casual way in which some people handle the Blessed Sacrament. He wonders whether the loss of reverence could have happened through the careless way we talk about Meal, Bread, Cup, without bothering to explain the way we use these words; that they are vocally capitalized must be clear that we are not speaking about any bread, any meal.

On the other hand, Kevin Seaholtz finds the regulation that Mass should not be celebrated in refectories or on tables ordinarily used for meals unfortunate. He believes that if Christians are to have a deep appreciation of the Eucharist as a meal, and if they are to realize the profound relationship that should exist between the liturgy and the rest of their lives, perhaps the occasional celebration in the refectory is one of the best ways to communicate these values. Both he and Michael O'Carroll agree that for most people small, white wafers do not look like food. The norm is insistent that if bread is to signify effectively the meaning it is intended to convey, it must really look like food. Experience has shown that loaves, other than small wafers are sometimes more appropriate, especially with small groups. Certainly as it is in most parishes, the form has become so spiritualized that one can almost speak of the danger of its being unrecognizable as bread. The Mass is a meal, an encounter, a vital relationship with Christ who took bread, broke it and said, "This is my Body."

It is obvious that the Council Fathers of Vatican II envisioned a controlled variety, allowing practically all liturgical forms. And it is this very freedom that vexes some. They feel that the old liturgy could have been kept for at least a time, and Loret notes

Mary Hester Valentine

that even among those who welcome the new Mass there are some who would like to return occasionally to the liturgical style of their childhood. Actually Masses in Latin with participation by the people are celebrated in various places from time to time. In fact, pilgrims at St. Peter's Basilica join in singing the *Gloria* and Creed, as well as *Sanctus* and *Agnus Dei* in Latin.

Report has it that the Irish church is notably traditional, but it was in a small town in Ireland that I witnessed an effort to include all ages and groups of parishioners. The bulletin in front of the Church announced the Sunday Masses, as I recall in this order: 7:00 Latin Mass, 9:00 English Mass, 10:00 Gaelic Mass, and 11:00 Guitar Mass!—an interesting distinction, since the last did not bother announcing the language. When I asked whether the early Mass, attracting the older parishioners, might not be in Gaelic I was informed, to my surprise, that it was the young who learned the language in school who were more fluent in the native tongue, and it was they who had requested it. I am sure that not all parishes in Ireland followed this pastorally oriented schedule, but it impressed me as a genuine effort to make the Mass "meaningful" to all the groups.

Which brings up the complaint one hears from traditionalists—those with enough time and money to travel abroad. They lament that they no longer feel at home at Mass when the language is a vernacular not their own. One wonders why they feel Catholics in the countries they visit should give up their language to accommodate tourists.

One can be an integral part of a worshiping community even when the cultural adaptations and language is unfamiliar. I recall sitting on the floor around a foot-high table altar in Korea, reciting from the "Romanization" of the Mass liturgy my Korean friend had given me: "*Wriju yesu Krisooe abeoji-isin cheonjuneun chanmi badeusoseo,*" (Christ, have mercy) and feeling the union in the Body of Christ that this liturgical gathering was inviting us all to share.

To the average parishioner the language of the Mass with which he has problems differs from that of the linguists and theologians who finally came to consensus. The formulas that have been introduced are from ancient times, probably the very words used at the blessing of bread and wine in the Jewish meal at the time of Christ, according to Jungmann. The renewed Offertory formula, for instance, embodies a three-fold idea: the bread and wine are products of this, our earth, and thus symbolize our world and our life; they also signify the work of our hands and our daily labor. Nor does he have any difficulty accepting the fact that the elaborate offertory rite that had developed over the course of the Middle Ages was set aside and brought back to its simpler origins.

The average layman's problem, quite frankly, is with the Liturgy of the Word. He has been told that the three readings from Scripture on Sunday emphasize the theme of the Mass, and he has difficulty finding any unity in the three. Even Basil Pennington admits that he was sometimes hard pressed to see a theme relating to all three readings until an English scholar who worked on the preparation of the lectionary informed him that it was only the first reading, the Old Testament, that was chosen in view of the Gospel. That being the case, some wonder why the New Testament second reading is included. An explanation would help here.

But the difficulty is more than finding a relationship in the readings. There are many occasions when one has a sense of being flooded with words, with no opportunity to grasp a phrase or thought to carry as a kind of *mantra* for the day or a direction for the week. A friend complained recently, "There are too many sacred words racing by; I can't focus." My admittedly inadequate defense was, "But in a short service a momentary distraction would mean the loss of the whole." The homily was intended to supply the bridge, but too frequently, it relates only faintly to the words just read.

Enough has been said about the discontent of

THE MASS

American Catholics with sermons, and I do not intend to go into that aspect here other than to note that non-Catholics also frequently "shop around," until they find a church and a pastor whose words of faith inspire them to a more Christ-centered life. Perhaps all seminaries should concentrate a bit more on the words of the Master, "Go, teach all nations," remembering that for any one to learn, a teacher must be listened to, and the content of his message needs to be reinforced by his own enthusiastic, convinced delivery.

Another area that cries for reevaluation is the translation used. Perhaps in an effort to make the Scripture "Good News for Modern Man," not enough time was allowed for those entrusted with the task of translation to view their work with a sufficiently critical eye. There is no need to return to the Douay or King James versions, since scholars question their accuracy at times, although the majesty of their translations carries a distinctive message. But surely the great miracle of the raising of Lazarus deserves better than, "Lazarus, come out here." A friend of mine called my attention to a responsorial verse which had the congregation shouting, "I will make water in the desert." One need not be a pedant to feel that this particular phrase has quite another meaning in America than the translators intended to put into the mouth of God.

Some Catholics have difficulty with the current

tendency to use Yahweh instead of God in many contemporary hymns, especially since the words of the Mass itself retain God and Lord. A friend remarked that she always addresses her personal prayer to God; she does not remember ever thinking Yahweh or using it. Another wondered what her Jewish friends thought of our frequent use of "that holy and awesome name of the Lord, YHWH," which to them remains secret and unpronounced. I became aware of the strong feeling about Yahweh when another friend told me she objected to it ever since she read the definition in her dictionary: "a modern transliteration of the Hebrew word translated Johovah—used by some critics to discriminate the tribal god of the ancient Hebrews from the Christian Jehovah." It is a small matter, but any irritant that takes the worshiper's attention from the Act is not a minor one.

There is some debate on the use of multimedia, but many agree that within the context of the liturgy of the Word it can be very effective. Even here it would seem that Kevin Seasoltz' warning is in order, "Improvisation in accord with pastoral needs ought never undermine the genuine character of the Church's worship."

Many scholars point out that the prayers of petition should not merely echo the readings and the homily that have just preceded (as in fact often happened in an over-hasty development before the

Council.) Neither should it become an occasion for the free improvisations of the participants' reactions, as might be the temptation at a Mass celebrated in a small group or in a home. Rather, it should be a prayer of petition for the Church and for the world. The Order of the Mass does, however, expressly make provision for the addition of special intentions. Chapungo notes that here, too, banality and vulgarity in the liturgy are absolutely offensive, not to say detestable. Liturgical language should always be noble and prayerful as befits the community's act of worship.

John Meagher in *The Truing of Christianity* is not sure that the revision of the solemn words before Communion, "Only say the word and I (rather than my soul) shall be healed," is particularly happy. He finds the thought "dizzy minded," adding that the notion that we are sick with something that God can cure by ceasing to withhold the right word is theologically outrageous."

In short, there is need for a revision of the prayers of the Mass which will be in touch with the minds of the living, as well as in touch with ancient sources. Better translations are sorely needed, for as Basil Pennington says, "Faith and devotion will not, and are not meant to enable one to identify with awkward English, poor phrasing, and bad grammar." And then, there are the feminists who would rewrite the whole liturgy and Bible to eliminate what they consider a gender bias throughout. This is a question too complex to discuss in a study this brief, and has been dealt with in a number of books on sexist language in Scripture for anyone interested.

Some liturgists, as noted earlier, look upon the decision to maintain the creed in its traditional position between the homily and the prayer of the faithful as a structural flaw. Their argument is that the homily is meant to mediate the Word of God to the assembled community, and to stir up a response of faith and trust, which is reflected in the prayer of the faithful. But when the creed is interjected between the homily and the prayer of the faithful, it fractures the unity of the rite.

One last difficulty relative to the community participation in the Mass, which I have heard on a good many occasions is the suggestion made by some liturgists that there be a brief period for reflection between the first readings and the responsorial psalm. The time suggested varies according to the diocesan norms, but it ranges from 30 seconds to "a minute or so." Clearly it is too brief a time for any meaningful related thought, and too long a time during which the Congregation waits for the reading of the Gospel.

One very welcome change for most Catholics is the shift in emphasis in the Mass for the dead. The pre-Vatican Requiem and traditional burial services were fairly gloomy, with *Dies Irae* (day of wrath) predominating. Today's Mass of resurrection can not take away the mourners' sense of personal loss, but it does direct their minds to the Paschal mystery and our personal hope of resurrection because of Christ's overcoming of death. It is comforting to be reminded that "Life is changed, not taken away."

Concelebration, which was the focus of prolonged debate in the Council, has been accepted with little difficulty on the part of the faithful, whatever the reaction of the clergy, partly, one suspects, because it does not concern the laity, and partly because it usually accompanies a fairly formal celebration and enhances the significance of the occasion for those in the pews.

Because in the majority of cases God's house, whether in medieval times or our own, was built by the contributions or labor of the faithful, churches also became our houses of prayer, and parishioners maintained an attitude of communal ownership. As a result, some of the architectural changes proposed by the Council, and the articles dealing with sacred art, met with unexpected controversy which has not entirely died down even today. Arguments for retaining the old altar against the wall, the marble altar rails, the stained glass memorial windows, a plethora of statues and thickets of votive candles became emotional, and in some cases almost led to a split in the parish. Those favoring the change frequently referred to the excesses, some of which were not a case in point in their own church, such as the wax statue of Pope Pius XII, fully vested, in St. Patrick's Cathedral, New York, or the Franciscan skeletons' clothed in their habits in an Innsbruck church. Those opposing change cited promises made for favors granted which the statues represented, and the incongruity of Danish modern furnishings in a neo-Gothic 19th-century church. Eventually, one suspects, the problems will be ironed out wherever they still exist.

Commenting on reaction to these articles of the *Constitution* Mc Naspy says, "There is a current feeling that it doesn't matter where the Eucharist is celebrated. In many ways it doesn't." Some liturgical celebrations that he found most personally moving took place in unlikely surroundings, like a spartan hotel room in Russia. He continues to explain that while a parish may not need an elaborate sacral building, it does not follow that the only remaining option is one of barn-like sterility. Yet even a barn can be turned into a place of worship.

Those fortunate enough to attend a Mass in summer at Weston Priory when the monastic chapel is too small to accommodate the crowds who come to celebrate with the monks, will agree with Mc

THE MASS

Naspy. The Weston Priory barn-Mass is one of prayerful solemnity and communal joy, an experience that lingers in the memory as a real participation in the Lord's Supper.

Mc Naspy also comments on the warmth of the small group liturgies in a home situation, with which by now most American Catholics are familiar. While approving (as who does not?) the advantages of intimacy and community felt in friendly, small groups, he questions whether there is not a danger of elitism or cliquishness when one's worship is carried out exclusively in the surroundings of friends, and asks whether the Christian does not belong to the wider community as well as to the smaller homogeneous ones. He concludes that the smaller informal place fills certain needs and expresses certain realities about Christian community, but so does the larger, somewhat more formal place, for as social beings and Christians, we belong to many communities, and always to express one or other of these is a diminishment. A recent book, *Shaping a House for the Church*, by Marchita Mauck, proposes that a church building must both reflect and form a people.

Articles 112-121 of the *Constitution on the Liturgy*, which deal with sacred music have probably elicited as much debate on the parish level as any other section of the document. Someone has suggested that this may be because this branch of the liturgy

was affected in its roots, even though the Prepara-
tory Commission took care to relegate the purely
technical consideration into the background, and to
emphasize the pastoral-liturgical side of the issue.
The Council Fathers stressed that sacred music,
since it is intimately linked with liturgical action,
express prayerfulness, solidarity, and a heightened
solemnity of the sacred rites.

The great masterpieces of music were to continue
to maintain their rightful place in worship, but it
should not be forgotten that the nobility of the
liturgy requires the active collaboration of the
people of God. It was acknowledged that the execu-
tion of Gregorian chant was beyond the power of
the average parish, and as a result, "other kinds
of sacred music, especially polyphony are by no
means excluded from liturgical celebrations, so
long as they accord with the spirit of liturgical
action (Art. 116).

Developing this concession, the document rec-
ommends composers to produce compositions
which have the qualities proper to genuine sacred
music, not confining themselves to works which
can be sung only by large choirs, but providing also
for the active participation of the entire assembly of
the faithful. This acknowledgment of a need for
new music stressed that the hymns be orthodox,
short, simple in text and tune, and that they be
created chiefly out of biblical psalms and chants,

avoiding the sentimental "devotional" manner that Abbott states has proved the bane of much Catholic hymnody.

It was an admirable and ambitious proposal, and if its aims have not yet been achieved, it must be admitted that recent hymnals are more in conformity with the norms than some of the earlier attempts which flooded Catholic musicology in the years immediately after the Council. Part of the problems may have been an unforeseen interpretation of Article 119 which admits that "in certain parts of the world, especially mission lands, there are peoples who have their own musical traditions, and these play a great part in their religious life." For this reason, importance was to be attached to this music and the traditional music promoted and encouraged.

The results of this authorization for diversity were unanticipated, one may presume, although Bernard Lee, S.J., points out that two-and-a-half centuries ago a musical struggle emerged within the faculty of St. Thomas school in Leipzig, a conflict between the school's cantor, Johann Sebastian Bach, and its rector, Johann August Ernesti. Ernesti believed the students should give more time to the critical study of the Scriptures, and sing less, while Bach thought faith and its musical expression were important. While this specific problem does not dominate the ecclesiastical musical scene in the

Mary Hester Valentine

United States, it was a foreshadowing of differing emphases in post-Vatican II hymnody. Folk music has been popular for the past several decades, and became the base for many hymns in the post-conciliar church. While they were enthusiastically received by some members of the congregation, an equal number of parishioners were unresponsive, if not actually turned off. I had a personal sense of alienation shortly after returning from a six-year period out of the country, when I attended a Mass during which the guitar-strumming young people sang con brio "One Tin Soldier," while Communion was being distributed. I had realized that the anti-Vietnam war protests were strong, but did not anticipate the activists being musically assimilated in the Mass. Mine may have been an isolated experience, but there is no question that much of the music produced immediately after the Council hit a low point. While much remains to be done in this area, things are much better, and this improvement has grown, at least in part, through the annual Symposia for Church composers, conceived and hosted by Archbishop Rembert Weakland. These gatherings bring together a group of liturgical scholars, practitioners and church composers to explore liturgical music in light of the conciliar reforms, and for the encouragement of new musical compositions.

While the guitar has come in for its share of criticism in some parishes, it is well to remember that stringed instruments: the lyre, the harp, the psaltery, the sackbut, the dulcimer have been used to praise God centuries before the organ was invented, even though the Council in Article 120 of the *Constitution on the Liturgy* states that the pipe organ is to be held in high esteem, since in the Latin church "it adds a wonderful splendor to the Church's ceremonies, and powerfully lifts up man's mind to God." And we ought remember that Mark tells us (Mark 14:26) that at the Last Supper, after singing hymns of praise they walked out to the Mount of Olives.

While there is no question that church music underwent a critical period as a result of 20th-century liturgical renewal, solutions are being found, and as our Protestant friends remind us, their soul-stirring hymnody took 400 years to develop.

One happy result of the directives on the involvement of the faithful can be observed in almost every church in North America on any Sunday. The day when a few timid voices joined in the singing is long past. Except for those who seldom or never sing on any occasion, the voices of the congregation are raised in praise and thanksgiving unto God. (Nehemiah, xii, 46.)

Another addition to certain festival Masses which was met with staunch supporters and equally strong dissenters has been the introduction of the dance. Mc Naspy, who has no problem with it, comments that, "The dance in liturgy may strike certain of my contemporaries as inherently blasphemous." He goes on to point out that the ritual solemnity of an old-style pontifical Mass was surely a stylized dance, and the liturgical dance at Seville has long been performed. He admits that it will take on different forms, according to the age and temperament of the congregation. But both dance and mime have been most effectively used in the cathedral in Oakland, California during summer liturgies for the young. One such dance included an abundance of balloons. He concludes that gesture, after all, "and dance, differ not so much in kind as in degree, and even a rigorist will not avoid all gesture."

That liturgical dance is not for all tastes would seem to limit its use to those occasions when a reasonably homogeneous congregation can be anticipated. Otherwise, what May Thibaudeau calls using the body as an instrument of prayer for the honor of God will produce the opposite reaction. One woman attending a Mass which included liturgical dance remarked, when asked if she did not find it impressive, "I felt as if I were watching the Vestal Virgins perform." Extreme? Yes, but that woman expressed the feeling of, perhaps, a good many of the parishioners.

Bishop Gaughan, no rigid traditionalist, certainly,

notes that "The period of balloons and strange gy-rations once was used to call attention to what we said should be joy in the liturgy." But, he points out that there is another kind of joy, a quiet joy that the community experiences when they stand in the presence of the mystery of God. Perhaps here, it is simply a question of compromise: when liturgical dance is to be a part of ceremony, the parishioners should know in advance, so that those who find it not to their liking can opt to attend another Mass.

The changes in the liturgical calendar, which oc-cupy an entire chapter in the document, have met with minor comments, if any, probably because unless one were named Christopher or Philemon, both having been dropped from the list of saints, the changes did not especially touch the lives of the ordinary layman. Actually, however, the adjust-ment of the liturgical calendar was an important change, since it attempted to rectify the obscurity to which the death-resurrection mystery had been rel-egated through the multiplication of feasts. The Eastern rites have long commemorated the Holy Mother of God. "Especially for our all holy, spot-less, most highly blessed and glorious Lady, the Mother of God and Ever Virgin Mary," the priest sings in the Mass, and this calls forth from the faithful an acclamation that is variable, but always ends with "you are truly Mother of God, you do we magnify."

Mary Hester Valentine

The Constitution further insists that while Christ is our one Mediator (1 Tim. 2:5) Mary has a true maternal role. In Article 103 the Commission inserted a clear statement, by mentioning the "inseparable bond with which Mary is joined . . . to the saving work of her Son." Marian piety in such a context certainly is acceptable, even from an ecumenical point of view.

Even older than the Marian feasts are those of martyrs, originally celebrated in the respective local churches. Feasts of other saints were soon added, and doctors of the Church, founders of religious orders, martyrs, and holy men and women from many times and countries. Some of the feasts date back to the time when a man or woman locally recognized as holy earned the title "saint" by popular acclaim. But even since the process for canonization was formalized by Pope Urban VIII in 1634, a multiplication of saints has continued. Even since the Council a goodly number of canonizations have taken place, but their feast days appear to be limited to the diocese and country where they lived and worked, thus maintaining the urgency expressed by the Council Fathers that the Eucharistic celebration should always be a memorial of the life and resurrection of Christ, never losing sight of the fact that it is not merely a pious memorial; it is a living reality.

THE MASS

Article 102 stresses the fact that in the cycle of a liturgical year the Church unfolds the whole mystery of Christ, not only from his incarnation and birth until his ascension, but also as reflected in the day of Pentecost, and the expectation of a blessed, hoped-for return of the Lord. In recalling the mysteries of redemption, the riches of Christ's powers and merits are opened to the faithful, "so that these are in some way made present at all times, and the faithful are enabled to lay hold of them and become filled with saving grace."

There is no question that the most important thing Christians have done since the Apostolic age is to celebrate the Eucharist. As Bernard Lee indicates, "In so doing they have understood better whence they came, who they are, and what they are called to become." Vatican II consistently reminds us that the communal character of our Christian worship implies a communal Christian life. The problem is that we have used the word community so thoughtlessly and glibly, applying it to so many situations which are not really communal, that it is difficult to define it in specific terms. Perhaps a hint of an answer is contained in the parable of the Good Samaritan (Luke X, 25-32), which Jesus gave the lawyer willing to justify himself who asked, "And who is my neighbor"? The ending of that incident is applicable: the neighbor is "he that showed mercy," and Christ's answer, "Go, and do the same," is a good foundation on which to build Christian community.

In the past, the social dimension of human life tended to be ignored in the multiplication of private pious exercises. Those old enough to remember Mass before Vatican II remember the recitation of the rosary, sometimes interrupted by the leader for the Consecration, the hearing of Confessions during some Masses on First Fridays, and in larger urban churches, several Masses being celebrated simultaneously at side altars with individual worshipers choosing which one to become involved in, even if it meant ignoring the parish Mass at the central altar. Church, whether Mass was being celebrated or not, was a place where one could pursue one's private devotions, and then leave to pursue one's individual, private life. The new Eucharistic ritual was devised in the hope of changing that attitude.

As John Egan stressed in *Liturgy and Justice*, Pius X taught us that the liturgy is the indispensable source of the Christian spirit; Pius XI taught us that the authentic Christian spirit is indispensable for social regeneration. And as a result, the liturgy is the indispensable source of Christian social regeneration. Our problem today, then, is to make our liturgy inclusive of the hopes and fears, sufferings and aspirations of today's world, for if the Eucharist were truly Eucharist to us, the Church, and we are the Church, would be making an enormous contribution in solving the problems of the world. The day of *God and me* is over, if it ever had any authentic Catholic base. St. Paul (I Cor. 12:12) tells the Christians of Corinth that all are members of one body, the Christ who is *now;* that is, as Lee elaborates, not only are the many one, but the one the many are is Christ.

If our attendance at Sunday Mass is to be more than a relic of a childhood memory of an obligation, it must link us with the Christ, and lead us to works of charity and concern, since he has made us all children of one Father. Our involvement in the problem of our world will not be easy; it is bound to make demands that are difficult to fulfill, sometimes even dangerous, but it will provide new challenges, and we may again become a people who can be identified because we love one another—not with the facile implications of the Love banners, but by the concern we show for our sisters and brothers all over the world. It is risky, but rewarding to be lured away from the lonely security of private faith. The true Christians down the centuries have taken that risk and experienced the attending satisfaction of belonging to the family of God. I have forgotten who it was who addressed a meeting I attended, and reminded us that committees accomplish little; individuals make the difference, especially when the individual is motivated by the grace and force of Eucharist.

It is true that each Eucharistic sacrifice will touch us in a different way, since existentially we are different from the person we were at the previous Mass. Osborne points out that that is one of the reasons a startlingly new liturgy will not inevitably speak to the moment. Part of the solution lies within our grasp to work at realizing the words spoken, and their relationship to our lives today. The other solution, as Robert Cabie and Mary Durkin, and I presume a score of others have suggested, is for the leaders in the Church to explain the tradition on which the new ritual rests, and the diversity it allows. The tasks for the future, asserts Durkin, still include overcoming disagreement on controversial positions and working out an agreeable liturgical form. The last chapter of this study will address some of these problems.

But it is wise to remember what Karl Rahner emphasized again and again, even when his theological conclusions were under a shadow: changes develop slowly and in certain circumstances collide with heavy resistance, even in the Church. And even when they succeed, they remain fused with remnants of tasks left uncompleted. His and my concluding thought in this study of the current

THE MASS

Eucharistic theological debate is that a thousand things in the Church do not suit us; this is perfectly plain. The question is, why should they have to suit us? If the Church had to be just precisely the way we would like it, what would every one else do?

THE MASS OF THE FUTURE

WHAT WILL Mass be like in the 21st century, or in the 25th, for that matter? It would be foolish for any one to attempt to reply to that question. That there will be a Eucharistic celebration no true Christian doubts, for Christ has promised to be with his own to the end of the world. The Scriptures bear witness to the Risen Christ, but it is the Eucharist which gives the Risen Christ to the faithful in the special memorial meal he himself instituted. So, this great sign of the living Lord, the sign by which we recognize him assures us that he will be with future generations as he has been with those of the past, as he is with us today.

Schillebeeckx has warned in *The Eucharist* that no one can ever anticipate history, although he concedes that all kinds of implicit tendencies betray that the future has been prepared in the past. Both the Old and the New Testaments point out our tendency to foretell future events on the basis of visible evidence. Elijah (I *Kings*, xviii, 41-45) during a time of drought pointed out a natural phenomenon, a little cloud like a man's hand with black clouds following accompanied by wind, ending in the great rain the little cloud foretold. And Christ, (*Luke*, xii,

54) noting the circumstances in his own day and ours by which men are able to prophecy on the evidence, tells his listeners that when they see a cloud in the west they know that a shower is coming.

So, while in a rapidly changing world, not only the technical world but the church world as well, we may risk surmising, on the basis of the direction the Church is facing in the present, where she may go in the future. Raymond Brown has pointed out that orthodoxy is not always the possession of those who try to hold on to the past; a truer criterion may be the efforts made to answer new questions, and to adapt to changing times without ever relinquishing the basic truths on which all rests. For surely, Bernard Lee is correct when he suggests that Christianity's potentiality will move to actuality only if the Eucharist is celebrated in a different way and with a different perspective than it ordinarily is today. He adds that we do not need to devise alternative forms of worship, but we do need to worship according to the alternative we have become in Christ. It is not novelties that are required, it is important to stress here, but a deeper understanding of the character, the structure and elements of the celebration, especially of the Eucharistic prayer, to enable the faithful to participate more fully, and with greater awareness.

Scholars have always worked within the intellectual climate of their time, and they may be influenced by currents of thought, although they do not always find direct expression in their writings. It is a question of a direction which they follow, the new horizons and perspectives which challenge them. The changes we have seen are the result of this as much, perhaps, as the local churches' attempts to follow the directives of the Constitution. On April 3, 1980, an instruction, *Inestimabile Donum*, was issued by the Congregation for Divine Worship. Its fundamental principle is that "the faithful have a right to a true liturgy," and warns that undue experimentation, changes and creativity bewilder the faithful. It goes on to suggest that anyone taking advantages of the reform to indulge in arbitrary experiments is wasting energy, and offending the ecclesial sense. Several theologians have agreed with this by stressing, as Kevin Seasoltz does that "changes that are too radical can be pastorally debilitating," adding, however, what has been the implementing issue ever since liturgists began to be concerned about the gap between the celebration of the Mass and the participants in the pews: provision must be made for progressive evolution of the Church's institutions. History teaches us that when the liturgy is not adapted to the times, does not respond to its demands, and lacks solid theological basis, lethargy and indifference are just around the corner.

THE MASS

Returning to Schillebeeckx we find the discerning remark that "The fact that today's modern language is dated tomorrow, simply implies that expressing the truth is a never-ending task which has to be begun anew all the time." Tomorrow, one suspects, the liturgy will be incomprehensible outside its anthropological and general theological framework. So far, one must admit that the post-conciliar liturgy has been flexible enough to admit variations according to different cultures, probably the most striking feature of today's Roman rite. Chupungo, expanding on this, stresses that the incarnation is an historical event, but its mystery lives on whenever the Church assumes the social and cultural conditions of the people among whom she dwells. Adaptation is not thus an option, but a theological imperative arising from incarnational exigency. Chupungo adds that the Church must incarnate herself in every race, as Christ incarnated himself in the Jewish race. He goes back to Vatican II to justify his position, pointing out that the procedure proposed by the Council is one of integration. This pluralistic view will not hurt the universality of the Church, for there can be no truly universal Church without truly local churches adorned with their own traditions. This implies certain accommodations on the part of the Christian liturgy; the best thing that can happen to the liturgy, since as no

113

culture is static, the liturgy will be constantly sub-
jected to modifications. In this sense the incarnation of the Church's worship will be an on-going
process whose basic content will remain unvaried,
but whose structure, language and symbols will
bear the mark of each culture. Liturgical pluralism
is, therefore, an incarnational imperative, rather
than a concession of Vatican II, and a borrowed rite
is an alien rite.

If one agrees with Chupungo and others both in
the Western and Eastern church, as it would seem
we must, perhaps our attempt to pierce the future
in regard to Eucharistic celebration should begin
with cultural diversity.

The question that confronts the Roman Catholic
church throughout the world, then, is how to bring
the Roman liturgy closer to the hearts of people
coming from diverse cultural backgrounds. Although we may have forgotten it, this is not new in
the history of the Church.

It is to the possible cultural adaptation of the
liturgy of the Eucharist that we will look first, since
some of this has been occurring even in the United
States. I have already referred to George Stallings, a
black priest based in Washington, D.C., who, early
in 1989, was suspended by his Archbishop after
having established what he planned to become the
mother church for African-American Catholic congregations. Defying archdiocesan orders he cele-

brated Mass with the splinter group known as the Imani Temple, blending traditional liturgy with gospel music and revival-tinged oratory. Within a year, having cut his ties with the Vatican, he was consecrated as the Congregation's first Bishop by Archbishop Richard W. Bridges, president of the Independent Old Catholic Churches of California, a group which split from Rome in the 1870s in a dispute about papal infallibility. The five attending Schismatic bishops were, interestingly enough, white.

Whatever one may think of Stalling's action, it put new pressure on the Church to reach out to its black members. The Milwaukee *Journal*, editorializing on Stallings' schism commented that "surely the church is secure enough to accommodate cultural and social diversity in its worship. And while only 1.5 million of the church's 53 million American members are black, it does not relieve Catholics of the obligation of making black members (or potential members) feel more comfortable. At the moment the discomfort level for blacks remains relatively high, and Stallings believes it will remain so as long as the Church reveres white European values over all others."

Without question Stallings did rock the boat, and his action has sent out waves, but the United States Conference of Bishops had already begun studying ways to accommodate liturgy not only to the cultural needs of Afro-Americans, but to Hispanics, Oriental-Americans, and others living and worshiping in our pluralistic society.

A national group of Black Catholic clergy committed itself at its 1989 meeting to a study of the development of an African-American rite within the Catholic church. The issue of such a rite is almost a century old, but Father Victor Cohea, a board member of the clergy caucus said this is the first time a group of black Catholics has proposed a study. Stallings certainly heightened the intensity of the issue. Real efforts are being made to come to grips with it.

For example, in April, 1990, SS. Gall and Elizabeth churches, longtime sister parishes in the inner city of Milwaukee, announced their preparation to become partners in a worship center to serve black Catholics in the Archdiocese. "The center is believed to be the first in the country developed by the deliberate policy of an archdiocese," said Brother Joseph C. Hager, director of the office of Black Catholic Concerns here.

The churches, separated by about seven blocks, but united in mission, will experiment with prayer, worship and sacramental celebration that is culturally African and theologically Roman. Organizers hope that many of the archdiocese's 12,000 black Catholics, only about 3,000 of whom are currently active, will be served at the two locations.

"Building renovations will include a fellowship

area which will include an ethnic Marian shrine," said Michael Krecji, pastor of St. Gall. The shrine will include a figure of Our Lady of Guadalupe to represent the Hispanic element of the parish, a figure of Our Lady of Perpetual Help to represent white parishioners, and a wall carving of an African Mary and Jesus, a gift from a couple who had gone to Liberia to work with lepers." At St. Elizabeth there is an increasing use of African art, vestments and altar linens. Sunday Masses at both churches are frequently longer, since it is not uncommon in black culture for Sunday Church attendance to take an entire morning or more.

The two churches have instituted a twice-yearly revival schedule. The Lenten revival held on five nights in spring of 1990 featured three guest preachers, seven guest choirs and the parish gospel choir. Mel Herman, pastor at St. Elizabeth, says he is learning a style of preaching that calls for involvement and response from worshipers, and is marked by increased feeling.

These changes would have been unheard of a quarter-century ago, probably even five years ago, but one suspects adjustment to indigenous needs will be in direct response to the experience-based sense of the American church.

Kevin Seaholtz, back in 1979, noted that indigenization is not an option, but a theological imperative. Liturgical pluralism is a necessary corollary to the Church's nature to be local. In the United States this means a response to the great variety of cultures present, and will include the new immigrants who are coming from Eastern Europe, Asia, Polynesia, and the Middle East. The Church must also attend seriously to the great cultural differences that extend from the urban centers on the East and West coast to the rural areas of the South and Midwest. It implies an awareness of cultural differences that distinguish mobile or migrant peoples from stable people who live in America's small towns and villages.

Happily, Vatican II deliberately left room for the adaptation of the liturgy to the genius and traditions of individual peoples (Art 40).

In many parts of the world liturgical reform and renewal will be viewed in the context of efforts to regain their cultural identity. Seaholtz points out that where Western liturgy has been imposed on people whose thought patterns and symbol systems are more Eastern than Western, the Church and her rituals have maintained an immigrant status. In the future, native liturgies, it is to be hoped, will provide the focus for religious identity, because they will enable people to join their own cultures with the heritage of Western theology and Roman liturgical patterns.

Unity, not uniformity will be the norm, and Vatican II assumes that the new Eucharistic model is to

THE MASS

be adapted to the particular genius of every culture. For example, prayer in one culture (Anglo-Saxon) may be sober and direct, in another, dramatic and elaborate. A Korean funeral for a dearly-loved Jesuit, an American who died after spending about a decade teaching in the University, lasted five hours, and none of the Korean participants indicated any desire to truncate what, to them, was a necessary tribute. Ordinarily, Koreans are a low-keyed people, but a ceremony, religious or otherwise, must give enough time to engage those participating.

The church of the future will include enculturation as well as acculturation. Bernard Lee explains that while acculturation modifies the ritual by using established cultural elements, enculturation attempts to change the culture by infusing its cultic ways with Christian symbols and myths. Its aim is to imbue the culture with the spirit of the Gospel. The Church has been doing this for centuries: changing ancient pagan feasts to Christian ones, utilizing harmless celebrations and adapting them to Christian usage. The feast of St. Peter and St. Paul on February 22 took the place of the Roman commemoration of the dead ancestors whose authority was represented by their chairs.

Creativity and adaptation characterized the liturgy, especially from the Edict of Milan to the 8th century. Her attitude during this period was one of respect for all that was good and noble in life. In many cases it replaced pagan cultic elements with Christian observances, being careful not to abolish something without putting something else in its place. Another example would be the suppression of the feast of the birth of the sun god in Mithraic religion, and the institution of the feast of Christmas in its place. The Christmas tree, the Easter egg, the Yule log, even St. Valentine's day come to mind as examples, but who other than a scholar of ancient cultures knows the origin of these few symbols?

But, as Karl Rahner notes, we have to admit that until now our brothers and sisters in lands outside the West have been treated, unintentionally perhaps, as under-aged children in a family. We have formed them in a scholastic theology, given them a Latin liturgy, built them neo-gothic churches in the Orient, had them singing European hymns, and given them European bishops, or native bishops chosen for them in Rome to European specifications. In the future this Westernization will be overcome. In music, consideration will be given to native musical forms: divergent scales, and rhythms of their own. Theirs will be a liturgy to which they can respond, because it will be their own.

Time and again the question of using native food and beverage for the Eucharist has been raised in regions where wheat and grapes are not grown, and importation has become prohibitively expensive. The use of wine becomes even more problematic in Buddhist countries where devout Buddhists take offense at the public drinking of alcoholic beverages. Religious culture has branded wine as a thing of vice, and the Christian cup of salvation has become a cup of division. The question is an open one, and was discussed at the Council, but no clear decision was made, but as studies continue to be made, some adaptation to the equivalent of bread and wine in Christ's Palestine will be accepted.

After a series of three All-India Liturgical Meetings the Commission for the liturgy approved a new rite in which readings from Indian scriptures regularly precede readings from the Bible, and in which, not just on Good Friday, but daily, all are prayed for. John Meagher in *The Truing of Christianity* noted that at the time his book went to press (1990) the Indian anaphora was still being stalled in Rome. But one suspects that these changes and others embracing India's ancient, highly sophisticated culture will inevitably be a part of the Eucharistic celebration there. I shall dwell on this a bit more in the section on ecumenical dialogue and the Eucharist.

The emphasis the *Constitution on the Sacred Liturgy* put on the celebration of the Mass as an act of communal worship has led us to a reconsideration of what constitutes a community, thinking which has meant an evaluation of the places in which we worship, diversity demanded by the needs of the community involved, which may produce striking changes in church architecture of the future. Obviously differences in size have existed for centuries: here in the United States large cities called for large churches to accommodate the number of parishioners. Small towns and villages built smaller houses of worship. Another American phenomenon—the immigrant population, especially in the 19th century, was reflected in so-called "national churches," sometimes built within a few blocks of each other. It was not unusual for a church serving Irish-Americans to be within walking distance of another serving German or French-Americans, and as Ellis Island accepted more Poles, Italians, Czechs, and others from predominantly Catholic countries, churches to serve them began to spring up. Their purpose, obviously, was to make it easier for the new citizens to retain their faith, since in these neighborhood churches the language of their origin helped give them a sense of community. As younger generations became attuned to the American way, and forgot the language of their ancestors these national churches became truly catholic and lost their national identity. I refer to them only to point out that small, distinct church communities are no new thing in the United States.

But it is not this type of community which many

THE MASS

Catholics desire today. The Council outlined the ideal by stressing that the Eucharist celebrated by the Bishop is the true image of the Church, since she "reveals herself most clearly when a full complement of God's holy people . . . exercise a thorough and active participation in the altar where the bishop presides in the company of his priests and other assistants" (Art 41). Under present circumstances, however, that ideal can be realized only rarely today. And as a result the large congregation of the diocese has been divided into parishes.

Many feel that the parish church no longer is a satisfactory option since it usually is a gathering of strangers, which obviously does not realize the ideal of a parish family. Jungmann, accepting the reality of the situation nevertheless believes that the Eucharist cuts through differences of age, ethnic background and state of life, and brings friends and strangers together into one community united in worship. It is, he asserts, St. Paul's definition of Christians, "neither Jew nor Greek, slave or freeman, male or female, you are all one in Christ Jesus" (*Gal.* 3:28).

But we must recognize that St. Paul was not dealing with a city parish which may number several thousand. As long as the congregations have the size they do, the possibility of direct participation remains limited. It is up to us, the community, to see that participation does not consist of adherence to outward details. To say that large numbers diminish the possibility of such unity is to close the mind to the evidence we have seen on TV of crowds united by a single ideal: recently, for example, the sudden rush to break down the Berlin wall, with thousands of Germans on both sides of the wall participating, the gathering of Chinese students demonstrating for democracy on Tiananmen square. Christ did not consider numbers a problem; he fed 5,000 (John VI: 5-13) when Philip warned him that "200 denarii worth of bread is not sufficient that every one of them may have a little."

So, while Jesus has compassion on the multitude as well as on the two or three gathered together in his name, it would be unrealistic to say that we, his 20th century disciples, find close relationship that simple. We do not stand before God, but as a community of people vitally and organically bound to one another in Christ. And while the introduction of the vernacular, new music, lay ministries, celebration facing the people has transformed our celebrational style, it remains to be proved that it has transformed our ecclesial awareness of our sense of solidarity with one another, let alone our sense of solidarity with those who are not of our class or nation or color.

So, as Osborne points out, a future Eucharistic ritual will have to deal with pluralism, the need for intentional communities, the participation of many different people in many different ministries, and most importantly, he insists that this future ritual will have to balance transubstantiation of bread and wine with transubstantiation of the assembly. Jungmann agrees that the question of the group Mass and the house Mass may be legitimately raised; since Vatican II several countries have been fostering the practice. He feels that in every congregation small homogeneous groups would like to celebrate the Eucharist together, and that their family spirit is bound to produce a liturgy which will be alive in a personal way through the contributions of the individual to the formulating of petitions, the offertory, the dialogue homily, and the sign of peace.

Bernard Lee defines such a group as an intentional community: one that is larger than a family, but smaller than geographically determined groups such as most parishes are. He sees the intentional community as the most faithful, both today and in the future, since it aids participants to swing between intradependence and extra-dependence. In his book *Alternative Futures for Worship* Lee sees intentional communities celebrating Eucharist together as the building blocks of the Church for today and the future. He reminds us that it was in house churches that early Christians worshipped, and points to the contemporary base communities of the South American church, the small Christian communities in the African church, and believes these are the kinds of communities upon which American Catholic life will be truly expressed.

John Westerhoff, in the same volume, finds intentional communities to be one of the most significant events in the post-Vatican Church, finding in these an awareness of Christ's message to his disciples at the Last Supper, "Do this in memory of me." Westerhoff continues, "Do what? Do what is necessary to become what I have begun to make you by this action, namely members of my body to be my presence in the world."

John C. Haughey, S.J., feels that while the North American Catholic Church has a growing number of intentional communities, relative to our Third World brothers and sisters, we have very few such communities. He predicts there will be a network of intentional communities growing into a parish, rather than a parish breaking itself down into smaller community units or network parishes as we see developing today in some dioceses. As Mary Durkin notes, in Latin America the basic Christian communities celebrate Eucharist geared to strengthening them as they struggle against injustice.

There are those who hold that whether the liturgy takes place in a store-front chapel, or a casa in a public housing high-rise as in Spanish-speaking sectors of New York, until acculturation with the larger unit has been achieved, the use of the native language and native traditions are obligatory.

Are small intentional communities an indication of what the church will be like in the future, and will their liturgical celebrations be the blue-print for Eucharist? As Yogi Berra once said, "I won't make any predictions, especially about the future."

Attractive as intentional communities appear to be, there are some theologians who have reservations about them. Jungmann states that if the service is to be the Eucharist Christ entrusted to his Church, its liturgical actualization cannot be left to the free, spontaneous improvisation of whatever group happens to be celebrating at the moment. He warns that pastors will have to be on their guard that such communities do not degenerate into snobbism or elitism, sectarianism or mere trendiness, and that, as house Masses celebrated in the homes of the well-to-do, or the homes of minority or foreign language groups, do not emphasize differences, whether social, ethnic or cultural. Father McNaspy, no conservative, wonders whether most Christians are equal to the demands frequently imposed by small group liturgies, and questions whether they should be the rule or the exception.

Dean Hoge of Catholic University, suggests that the emphasis on celebrating as a community may have contributed to a strengthening of individualism, by identifying community with various comfortable ways of being together with one's own kind. There is no question that the smaller, informal place fills certain needs, but so does the larger, more formal place. As social beings, especially as Christians, we belong to many communities, and as Mc Naspy points out, "Always to express simply one or other of these is a diminishment, and possibly an evasion of responsibility.

Even in small group Eucharist, there will be different needs and different personalities, not all of whom can be satisfied. One responds easily to symbols, another only to ideas, and even within the individual, spiritual participation fluctuates between alert and joyous periods and times of indifference and dullness. As Romano Guardini noted years ago, "God's sacred act is planted in human imperfection."

One aspect of the Eucharist we can be reasonably sure is a trend which will be developed still further in the future is a greater attention to the needs of children, with special Masses composed for them. In 1973, Pope Paul VI ordered a liturgy to accommodate the capacity of the young participants. The opening will be simpler; there will possibly be only one reading, and that one a paraphrase to bring the Gospel message within their comprehension. As Basil Pennington notes, children need to know they belong. While geared to the needs of children, parents will be involved in a unique way. Those who have been present at the children's sermons in Rome on the Feast of the Holy Innocents know how every parent listens to the children. Pope Paul VI's mandate is aware of this and states, "Adults can also benefit spiritually from experiencing the part which the children have within the Christian community. "The kingdom of heaven is theirs; the heavenly places in which we celebrate, and since the kingdom is theirs, they can give it to us."

Orthodox Christians have always worked on the principle that the three sacraments of initiation are intimately bonded: baptism, Confirmation, and Eucharist. So, children receive their first Holy Communion at their baptism, and are welcome to the table of the Lord from then on. This was once a universal practice in the Church, but was lost in the West; it may be revived in the future.

I cannot leave this attempt to look into the future of the Eucharistic celebration without touching upon one of the most serious problems facing the Church of today, and so far as one can foresee, the Church of tomorrow, and that is the shortage of priests. NCR on May 4, 1990, addressed the problem of the dramatically declining number of priests and seminarians, the aging priesthood with 50% over 65.

On November 30, 1989, Archbishop Rembert G. Weakland discussed the issue at length in his column, "Herald of Hope," in the Archdiocesan paper, *The Catholic Herald*. Says the Archbishop, "I have put the phrase 'priestless Sundays' in quotes because I am not fond of the expression, even though it has become standard usage as a way of talking about parishes and faith-communities that come together to worship on Sundays when there is no priest to celebrate Mass. Thus the phrase should logically be, 'Mass-less Sundays'."

He goes on to say that the bishops at their last meeting went over a document on this phenomenon that had been prepared by its Liturgical Committee as an aid to understanding what is happening across the country, (51 dioceses reported that they have cases now of parishes where no priest is available for Sunday Mass). It was clear during the meeting that this kind of theological analysis must continue.

The primary question that had to be asked: "Is it better for a parish to stay together as a group and worship together on Sunday without Mass, or is it better that the parish disband and parishioners be dispersed to other parishes, especially if the latter are not too far away?

"A recent document from Rome on this question made it clear that the latter solution was presupposed, but no theological explanation was given, nor any rational discussion offered as to how far away neighboring parishes had to be, nor how inconvenient to get to them. Alternatives were not even raised. There is, however, much wisdom to the thought that a parish that has been in existence for some time should stay together and worship together—as it works, at the same time, to foster vocations. Further discussion of this point is necessary. It is simply not easy to tell parishes to go out of existence when the faithful have spent so much time and energy in building up a faith community.

"The Roman document presupposes, also, that the obligation to attend Mass on Sunday is the highest value, more than the importance of keeping the faith-community together." This, too, Archbishop Weakland feels, needs much further analysis.

He explains that the U.S. document does not enter into the whole question of this obligation and dispensation from it, in those cases where no Mass is available. He notes that "Bishops who have been experimenting with situations where there is no Mass on Sunday do not explicitly tell their people in those parishes that they are dispensed from the Sunday obligation, although it seems that this must of necessity be done. A bishop does not have the power to substitute as an obligation a service that is not a Mass."

He goes on to say that the bishops approved a document called an "Order for Sunday worship without Mass." This rite is to be used if there is no

Mass, and can be done in one of two ways: as a liturgy of the Word, followed by distribution of Communion, or the liturgy of the hours with the rite of distribution at the end. He comments, "I feel positive that the former will be used 95% of the time. It is what people know; it is what is readily available; it is what looks like a Mass." But he points out, "There are some inherent dangers in using Sunday after Sunday something that looks like a Mass but isn't a Mass. Jokingly, some bishops referred to the fact that people said they liked Sister's Mass better than Father's Mass. (It may well have been better prayer and liturgy, but betterness does not raise a non-Eucharistic service into a Mass.)

"There are few liturgists and theologians out there who wonder whether it would be preferable, when no Mass is possible, that there also be no distribution of Communion, and nothing that looks like an ersatz Mass. This is a valid question. Is abstinence from Eucharist better under such circumstances?

"There are several reasons for asking the question. Communion outside the Mass, in the oldest and most solid Catholic tradition was reserved for those who were dying. It was never meant for just the convenience of the faithful whose time schedules could not permit attendance at Mass.

"The Catholic tradition does not support massive distribution of Communion just because no Mass is available. From a psychological point of view, it could also be asked if abstinence from receiving Eucharist would not also be a better way of forcing the entire church to address the question of the shortage of clergy, rather than looking to theologically weak substitutes.

"Finally, there is the danger—one which I have seen occur elsewhere in the world that confronted the problem in this way—that what should be an extraordinary solution becomes normative and ordinary. We are a Eucharistic church, and that word here means the celebration of the Sacrifice of the Mass, not the reception of Communion outside of Mass.

"These questions are serious and profound, and the bishops were aware of the many issues facing them by the approval of the new 'Order' when no Mass is available." Archbishop Weakland concludes by stating, "It became evident to me in so many ways that our faithful have been well instructed; we have done a good job. We are indeed a Eucharistic people, and we want no substitutes that might turn us into something else."

On January 10, 1991, Archbishop Weakland went further in a 6,000-word first draft of a pastoral letter to the faithful of the Archdiocese of Milwaukee. In it he notes that "God has given our generation a special challenge as we plan for the future of our local church," stressing that "We are a Eucharistic church. We are formed into a Faith community by a gathering around the table of the Word and the Eucharist." He goes on to state that "It is also evident that by the turn of the century we will have more parishes without a resident priest and with a lay administrator or a permanent deacon as administrator."

Then in a carefully qualified statement, which in no way is meant as a defiance of Pope John Paul, Archbishop Weakland says, that if certain parish conditions are met in a priestless parish, "I would be willing to help the community surface a qualified candidate for ordained priesthood—even if a married man—and, without raising false expectations or unfounded hopes for him or the community, present such a candidate to the Pastor of the Universal Church for light and guidance." He adds that he sees no other solution to the shortage of priests.

The United States is experiencing a shortage of priests later than some European countries. One of the first remedies throughout France to the growing shortage was the "circuit rider" approach. Priests traveled to many churches on week-ends, presiding over as many Eucharists as they could. When this led to increased clerical coronaries and breakdowns, bishops left priests stationary and put parishioners on wheels. People were invited to travel to regional churches, but the elderly and those with small children obviously could not.

THE MASS

In Germany the priest shortage has also raised important questions. Is ordination necessary for building up faith community? Has the importance of celibacy been exaggerated? As early as 1971, 71% of Austrian priests recommended ordination of married men of proven pastoral skills, and recent polls have shown that the Swiss prefer married priests to lay pastoral helpers.

A recent letter to the editor of the *National Catholic Reporter* perhaps inelegantly but accurately comments that it is stupidity for the Church to be rigid and picky about rubrics and experimental liturgy, overlooking the threat of losing the liturgy entirely. It is certain that the future Church is going to have fewer ordained priests, and any description of a future Eucharist must take account of this. The final report of *Parish Life in the United States* indicated that "it is increasingly likely that there will be but one priest in a parish, or in a growing number of cases, no full-time resident pastor," and Osborn sees it as incredible that while an increasing number of Catholics see the handwriting on the wall, not much seems to be happening to prepare for this situation. Bernard Cooke points out that "A liturgical crisis is already upon us that will grow more severe in the immediate future."

His suggested solution is similar to that proposed by Schillebeeckx in 1978, who admits that the church in the past laid down specific requirements with respect to ministry. But, he argues, these requirements had been, but should not be absolutized; alternative ministry practices are needed in the contemporary church, and are possible from a biblical and historical point of view. The early church, according to Schillebeeckx had no set rules about who presided at Eucharist. There were a great number of house communities in which the host presided over the Eucharistic celebration. The principle point he makes is that Catholic communities must somehow, as body of Christ, have the ability, the right, and the responsibility to celebrate Eucharist.

Bernard Cooke pursues the idea that there is no need for mediators to link the community with Christ. "If a community recalls Jesus, it recalls Jesus; if it praises God as Jesus and their Abba, it does praise God; if it is grateful and says so, that is what is happening." Clearly in some cases it is not doing it officially, but he questions whether the lack of official means that substantially the action is not occurring, or can a given community provide its own Eucharist, a leadership without officially designated minister?

Note: this is an option which he questions; he is not saying this is the absolute answer.

Cooke also wonders whether a rhythm of Eucharistic celebrations less frequent than every Sunday might not be sufficient. It may well be that daily Mass has become for us the accepted thing, and a matter of course, because other forms of raising the heart to God have become too lifeless or rigid, or have been neglected or insufficiently developed. Rahner lays down the norm that Mass is to be celebrated as often as this contributes to the glory of God and the benefit of man; other conditions, being of course, presupposed.

Obviously the quality of the Masses would be more important than simply their number, and Cooke suggests alternating eucharistic and non-eucharistic liturgies, adding that "it might lead to greater appreciation of Eucharist," but would isolate the faithful from the liturgical year.

We need only look back to Tudor England when saying Mass might lead to death on Tyburn, and attending the service meant a stiff fine with time in prison. Yet the Mass was performed and sacrifices made, including martyrdom; prices paid for what was deemed valuable enough for the suffering to be acceptable.

Irish Catholics remember with affection their hedge priests, who also, at the risk of their lives, traveled up and down the land to celebrate mass for a frightened but determined faithful. And in our own century, even on our own continent, priests like Father Pro, S.J., continued to say Mass whenever it was possible, even though it was forbidden by Mexican law. People gathered to join with him. He died, it will be remembered, crying, "Long live Christ, the King," when he was captured and executed for his "crime."

With the primacy of the Mass at stake it seems possible that some of the reasons for the shortage of priests, based upon regulations, shaky tradition not dogma, might be changed. Disciplinary rules have been changed before, some time-honored ones within the memory of many of us: the laws of fast and abstinence during Lent, the complete fast from Midnight on or before Communion, eating of meat on Fridays, and the Sunday Mass requirement fulfilled by a Saturday evening Mass.

The law of celibacy might be changed, since obviously, it is not *per se* an absolute requirement for priesthood, only a custom in the Roman rite. We already recognize the validity of Orders of Uniate priests, and others of the Eastern rites; we have married priests serving in the United States: Anglican and Lutheran converts who were married before their ordination as Roman Catholic priests. It is only fair to note that this step was not made easy for them, in spite of the Rome-approved program known as the "Pastoral Provision," the unprecedented invitation to the priesthood for the already married convert. In her book, *Married to a Catholic*

THE MASS

Priest, Mary Vincent Dally tells of the resentment, rejection, religious politics, scandal, and precarious financial difficulties surrounding the decision until, after five years of struggle, her husband, Peter Dally, was finally ordained and assigned as Associate Pastor at Holy Family Cathedral, Tulsa, Oklahoma.

Perhaps, too, it is time to look at the possibility of part-time priests, who would be available to celebrate Mass and administer the sacraments, while engaged in other work or professions. The priest-worker movement earlier in this century was an experiment that failed, but its very failures can serve as warning signals in drawing up a new program for part-time priests.

And then, there are the numerous ex-priests, some of whom have bonded together in the society, CORPUS, an association of those who want to be able to be active leaders in the Church, and who hope to be re-instated at some future time.

There remains the burning question which can not be avoided in this context: the ordination of women. A recent meeting at Notre Dame called for a re-opening of this hitherto closed issue. Two Bishops were participants: William Mc Manus and Kenneth Untener. A third, Thomas Gumbleton was present but did not speak. Both participating bishops spoke favorably of further study of current objections. Bishop Mc Manus even warned that the church's tradition of a male-ordained priesthood may be threatening the survival of another more important tradition: the centrality of Eucharist, and he noted that the dilemma provides reason for profound scholarly and open-minded reinvestigation of the reasons behind the church's tradition of a male-ordained priesthood and its position of excluding women. Bishop Unterer raised the theological question about Rome's assertion that the priest acts "in person of Christ," and therefore must be a male. He pointed out that some contemporary theologians agree that the phrase was mistranslated and actually means, "in the presence of Christ."

Raymond Brown, commenting on the statement that there were no women priests in New Testament times, notes that since in the New Testament the term "priest" is applied to Christians only in the broad sense of the priesthood of the people (1 *Pet* 2:5; *Rev.* 5:10), a priesthood of spiritually offering one's life as a sacrifice according to the demands of the gospel, it would seem, warranted to affirm that the term priest was just as applicable to women as it was to men in New Testament times. He goes on to say that if the more precise claim is made that women did not celebrate the Eucharist in New Testament times, there is simply no way of proving that, even if one may doubt that they did. We know very little about who presided at the Eucharist in New Testament times. Yet there is evidence that prophets did (*Acts* 13:2) and certainly there were women who prophesied (I *Cor* 11:5; *Acts* 21:9).

Elizabeth Johnson goes further when she notes that there is strong evidence for a vigorous ministry of women as colleagues with men in the early decades of the church: as teachers, prophets, apostles, missionaries, preachers, healers, speakers in tongues, and leaders of house churches. She adds that scholars are now trying to piece together what forces brought this public ministry of women in the early church to a diminished state.

Bernard Cooke underscores both Brown's and Johnson's statements when he says, "Over the centuries the fact that there were no women priests only proves that over the centuries there were no women priests." And Kevin Seasoltz adds that "it seems likely that they (women) will not only rightly claim, but also be given a fuller role in the Church's worship in the years ahead."

While a daily newspaper is not usually cited as a scholarly source, I found it interesting that while I was writing this chapter the Milwaukee *Journal* carried an article on the translation from the Italian of Giorgio Otranto's book on women priests. Otranto, according to the news item, is professor of classics and Christian history at the University of

Mary Hester Valentine

Bari, Italy. According to the *Journal,* he believes he has evidence that women served as priests in the early Christian church. He cites a fifth-century papal letter ordering a stop to the ordaining of women as priests. His evidence includes a mandate by Pope Gelasius I in the fifth century, an inscription on a tomb of a woman, Leta, who is identified as a *presbytera.* He also refers to similar inscriptions referring to the priestly ministry of women. He quotes Bishop Atto of the 9th century, who rightly or wrongly, held that in the ancient church both men and women were ordained to the priesthood.

Whether or not the learned Italian scholar is right is not my point here. What I found interesting was that this unusual bit of church history made its way into the daily paper next to articles of current importance: the Zebra mussel catch in the Great Lakes, the illegality of the suicide machine. The issue of the ordination will not simply disappear, and its implementation may help to solve the possibility of liturgical starvation.

Women now are participating in the ministry as assistant pastors, and in several dioceses as Vicars. One woman at a symposium in Rome composed of delegates from the UN and missionaries, during the "year of the Woman," reported that two Sisters of her Congregation lived and served in the Amazon

THE MASS

bush country, where priests came only infrequently. The two Sisters baptized babies, witnessed marriages, held the hands of the dying and prayed with them, but could not administer the consoling Sacrament of the sick, served as councilors, but could not give the peace of absolution to the troubled souls who came, and held Communion services for as long as the pre-consecrated hosts lasted. She ended by asking, "Who was discriminated against, the Sisters who could not be ordained, or the people of God to whom they could not give the complete comfort of the Church?"

It is a question that needs to be asked again and again.

I would like to close this peering into a possible future by referring briefly to the ecumenical movement and its influence on the celebration of the Eucharist in the future. When Pope John XXIII on January 25, 1959, announced his intention to call an Ecumenical Council he said it would be "not only for the spiritual good and joy of the Christian people:" he desired "to invite the separated Communities to seek again that unity for which so many souls are longing in these days, throughout the world." At the Council, to which he had invited delegates from Protestant and Orthodox Churches, he had them seated in St. Peter's across the aisle from the cardinals. In the Discussion of the Con-

stitution for the Liturgy the dialogue frequently stressed what liturgical renewal could mean. It would take us too far afield to discuss the document on Ecumenism in any detail, but it is relevant to note that Article 2 states unequivocally that "In his Church Christ instituted the wonderful sacrament of the Eucharist by which the unity of the Church is both signified and brought about," and a little further on goes even further by saying, "Little by little, as the obstacles to perfect ecclesiastical communion are overcome, all Christians will be gathered in a common celebration of the Eucharist."

As a result of the document, ecumenical commissions were set up in many dioceses, and the United States bishops while still in Rome at the third session, established a national ecumenical commission with Cardinal Lawrence Shehan of Baltimore as chairman. Within a few months, the commission had set up eight subcommissions to explore possibilities of formal conversations with Orthodox, Protestant, and Jewish bodies. As a result, extraordinary advances were made in the theological area of the Eucharist in a very short time. As Leonard Swidler notes in his summary of these dialogues, in his book which is required reading for anyone interested in this facet of current ecumenism, *The Eucharist in Ecumenical Dialogue,* "these bi-lateral consultations reveal quite startling general agreement in regard to the questions of ministry and Eucharist."

To summarize briefly: the consultation between the disciples of Christ and Roman Catholics stated, "We have discovered that our understandings of the Lord's Supper are more similar than we had expected." The Lutheran-Catholic consultation noted that concerning the Eucharist as sacrifice and the real presence of Christ in the sacrament, "we are no longer able to regard ourselves as divided." The international Anglican-Roman Catholic consultation expressed a near total theological agreement; there was substantial agreement on the doctrine of the Eucharist, and it no longer constitutes an obstacle to unity. The Roman Catholic-Presbyterian-Reformed consultation in the United States recommended that proper steps be taken to have the appropriate organs of both respective churches at the highest level officially affirm in some appropriate way that Christ is present and at work in the ministries and Eucharist of each tradition. Illustrative quotations, Swidler indicated, could be multiplied from the same and other consultations. What he found striking is not only the number of different statements attesting to shared doctrines, but the constant repetition of almost the very same language, suggesting that in this key area of doctrine, previously so disputed, the shared understanding is not only broad, but also extraordinarily deep. Considering its history, it is remarkable, too, that in many of the consensus documents, and in the requirements for a non-Catholic to receive the Eucharist in the Catholic Church, no mention is made of transubstantiation. Belief in the real presence is a requisite, but the how of this presence is not a demand. This official stance indicates that today one need not hold an intrinsic link between the two. In other words, the door is open to alternative theological explanations of the real presence.

It would be naive to project an immediate union of all churches, and intercommunion a possibility within the next year or two. But the first steps have been taken. Already in 1972 Bishop Elchinger of Strasbourg permitted couples of mixed marriages in his diocese, under specific conditions, to share in each other's Eucharist. In December, 1973, the regional Lutheran church reciprocated Bishop Elchinger's action, and Swidler notes, "Rome has not repudiated the action." For those who yearn for the day when Christians will be united, these first steps are encouraging. There are clearly many theological, historical and metaphysical nuances to be cleared before this is an actual fact.

Some years ago, Concordia Lutheran College of Milwaukee, gave an honorary degree to the distinguished Church historian, Kenneth Scott La Tourette, whose seven-volume history of the expansion of Christianity had just been completed. Representatives from church-related Wisconsin colleges and universities were invited to attend the testimonial dinner. I was one of the guests at that gathering and remember the white-haired scholar going to the podium after the meal to address us. I do not have his exact words, but no one who was there will ever forget their intention and meaning. He thanked us all for being there, and then went on to rejoice that ecumenism had made great progress in the last few years. In substance he said, "Twenty-five years ago this Lutheran Institution would not have given me, a Baptist, an honorary degree. And even if their courageous president had dared to risk the disapproval of his colleagues and done so, he would not have considered inviting you to this meal of fellowship." His glance covered the hall, stopping briefly to smile at tables where Roman collars were predominant, or where we veiled nuns were seated. Then he continued, "But supposing he had broken all precedents and invited you, I question whether you would have dared to accept the invitation. So, we have come a long way, a long way—but we have many miles still to go. We gather here to eat a fellowship meal, but we continue to forbid all but our own congregations to participate in the Lord's supper. I would like to remind you all that it is not *our* supper for which we set down conditions, and make restrictions. It is the Lord's supper, and he rejects no one."

Perhaps it is that universal Eucharistic celebration toward which the future is moving, following the exhortation of the Council which urged all the faithful "to recognize the signs of the times, and to take an active and intelligent part in the work of ecumenism. The concern for restoring unity involves the whole Church, faithful and clergy alike. It extends to every one" (*Decree on Ecumenism*, articles 4-5).

CONCLUSION

AS I noted earlier in this book, some observers at Vatican II were surprised that the opening sessions addressed matters of liturgical reform. It is now widely recognized, however, that the guidelines issued by the Council for a general restoration of the liturgy did more to change the face of the church and individual experience within it than any other resolution.

We have seen that the ideal form of celebrating Mass will never be found. History has shown that one form that meets all claims cannot be developed by initiative from below or by dictation from above, as Jungmann stresses. It is a task that must remain forever unfulfilled. All we can hope to achieve is the continuous compromise that approximates the unattainable ideal. There is always a need to be very careful that we do not imply that the way things were done was wrong, and the newly introduced ways are right.

As Elizabeth Johnson reminds us, like the Christians of the first century, we, too, are being called to write the good news in an idiom suitable to our time and place. Like them we are living disciples, and need to be about the never-finished business of

149

confessing Jesus Christ in a pilgrim church. We must claim Christ, so that a living Christology will be handed on to the next generation into the 21st century.

He will come to us, will be with us, will fortify us, and whatever tomorrow may bring, it will be of his sending. Ellen Pellegrin, in an unpublished manuscript sums it all up. "The Mass is a mystery; the people who come together at Mass are a mystery; it is God who is the source of both of these mysteries. The idea of full, conscious, active participation has to do with the relationship between the Mass, the people, and God. The idea is exciting. We have a part to play."

I wonder if any of us can begin to envision what the ramifications are for full, conscious, active participation. I even wonder if those involved in Vatican II saw the vision clearly, or is it possibly the vision of the Spirit?"

DISCUSSION QUESTIONS

1. How is the celebration of Eucharist central to Christianity?
2. Why are the current prayers of the Mass so similar to the prayers of the Jewish seder?
3. Do the formularies found in the synoptic gospels and Paul's epistles demonstrate that stylization of the Eucharistic liturgy had already set in, or is their another possible explanation?
4. When did the term transubstantiation come to be used, and why was it considered an apt expression for Eucharist?
5. What is the significance of the current debate in Roman Catholic theology over transubstantiation vs. transignification?
6. How do you respond to the Orthodox churches which are content to speak of Eucharistic change without a narrow definition of its nature?
7. If the Mass is an act, "Do this in memory of Me," why are there so many words?
8. How does the Constitution on the Liturgy change the Eucharistic emphasis from that promulgated by the Council of Trent?
9. How is doctrine explained in liturgy?

10. How would the fact that post-conciliar Catholics give equal emphasis to the Eucharistic meal and the Eucharistic sacrifice be reconciled? Are both dimensions legitimate?

11. How is the Eucharist simultaneously sacrifice and sacrament?

12. Why does the Church emphasize cultural adaptations?

13. Has the Eucharistic liturgy of Vatican II addressed the cultural needs of your parish?

14. Why was Communion under both species restricted after the Council of Trent, and restored after Vatican II?

15. Why was the reception of Communion apart from Mass discouraged by Vatican II?

16. Is it generally accurate to say that Roman Catholic theology has emphasized the Eucharistic presence of Jesus to the detriment of his other presences?

17. How is liturgy a social as well as a religious experience?

18. What does Bernard Cooke mean by saying that any given Eucharist is not the actions of humans in general, but a particular group with specific meanings for one another?

19. Does today's emphasis in the Eucharistic celebration reflect the Apostolic Age?

20. The New Testament is silent regarding the competent minister of the Eucharist. How is

the celebration described in *Acts* and early patristic writing?

21. Are the problems relative to the ordination of women doctrinal or traditional?

22. Avery Dulles discussing intercommunion across confessional lines states that Eucharist is not and never can be the sign of a perfectly achieved unity; it is always the sign of an imperfect unity seeking to become more perfect. Explain both what he means and why it is so.

23. Look through the prayers of the Mass and note how many times the Congregation says *Amen*. To what specifics do they give assent by so doing?

24. How can individuals make the liturgy relate to their lives?

25. In what way does the Church emerge continuously from the celebration of the Eucharist?

SOME HELPFUL READING

Bausch, William J., *A New Look at the Sacraments*. Fides/Claretian, 1973.

Brown, Raymond E., *The Community of the Beloved Disciple*. Paulist, 1979.

Cabie, Robert, *The Church at Prayer*, Vol. II, *The Eucharist*. Liturgical Press, 1986.

Chapungo, Anscar J., OSB, *Cultural Adaptation of the Liturgy*. Paulist Press, 1982.

Cooke, Bernard, *Sacraments and Sacramentality*. Twenty-third Publications, 1983.

Cwiekowski, Frederick J., *The Beginnings of the Church*. Paulist Press, 1988.

Dally, Mary Vincent, *Married to a Catholic Priest. A Journey in Faith*. Loyola University Press, 1988.

Durkin, Mary, *The Eucharist*. The Thomas More Press, 1990.

Egan, John J., *Liturgy and Justice: An Unfinished Agenda*. Liturgical Press, 1983.

Every, Feorge, *The Mass: Meaning, Mystery and Ritual*. Our Sunday Visitor, 1978.

Jungmann, Josef A., S.J., *The Mass. A historical, theological and pastoral survey*. Liturgical Press, 1970.

THE MASS

Lee, Bernard J., ed., *Alternative Futures for Worship*, vol. 3: *The Eucharist*. Liturgical Press, 1987.

Loret, Pierre, *The Story of the Mass*, translated by Sister Dorothy Marie Zimmerman. Liguori Publications, 1985.

Meagher, John C., *The Truing of Christianity*. Doubleday, 1990.

O'Carroll, C.S.SP., *Corpus Christi: An Encyclopedia of the Eucharist*. Glazier, 1988.

Pennington, Basil, *The Eucharist Yesterday and Today*. Crossroad, 1984.

Schillebeeckx, E., O.P., *The Eucharist*. Sheed and Ward, 1968.

Seasoltz, Kevin, *New Liturgy, New Laws*. Liturgical Press, 1979.

Swidler, Leonard, *The Eucharist in Ecumenical Dialogue*. Paulist Press, 1976.

The Documents of Vatican II, edited by Walter H. Abbott, S.J. American Press, 1966.

Worship. Collegeville, Minnesota.